Mikal Heggelund Foslie

Contribution to Knowledge of the Marine Algae of Norway

Mikal Heggelund Foslie

Contribution to Knowledge of the Marine Algae of Norway

ISBN/EAN: 9783337248499

Printed in Europe, USA, Canada, Australia, Japan

Cover: Foto ©ninafisch / pixelio.de

More available books at **www.hansebooks.com**

Contribution to Knowledge

of the

Marine Algæ of Norway.

By
M. Foslie.

I.
East-Finmarken.
With 3 Plates.

[Reprinted from Tromsö Museums Aarshefter. XIII.]

Tromsö.
Tromsöpostens printing office, by M. Astad.
1890.

Contribution to Knowledge of the Marine Algæ of Norway.

By

M. Foslie.

I.

East-Finmarken.

(With 3 Plates.)

The marine Flora along the coast of East Finmarken has, as far as I know, not formerly been investigated, nor has anything about it been published, except that Gunnerus in his Flora Norvegica mentions a couple of species found at Vardö. And the late J. E. Areschoug received a few algæ from collectors there. Cp. Aresch. Obs. Phyc.

The following List is founded on investigations made by supply from the University at Kristiania in the years 1882, 1887 and 1889, respectively in 5, 8 and 6 weeks. Of course, it is impossible in proportionally so short a time to investigate even tolerably exactly so wide a coast with several deep fjords. Best inquired is the litoral vegetation at Berlevaag and Mehavn, and partly the sublitoral zone at the latter place. I have visited the following places: Sværholt,

Lebesby, Kjöllefjord, Mehavn, Gamvik, Omgang, Finkongkjeilen, Berlevaag, Syltefjord, Havningberg, Vardö, Kiberg, Ekkerö, Vadsö, Nyborg, Bugönæs, Kirkenæs, Kjelmö, Pasvig and Smaaströmmen at Jakobselv. It is, however, to be remarked, that the stay at some of these places has been only for a few hours, at others for a couple of days. Much time is lost in moving by boat and steamer from place to place. As some algæ disappear early in the summer, and others only at that time bear reproductive organs, I had to visit the western as well as the most eastern part of the district as early in the season as possible, and afterwards to go back later in the summer to the same place, or an adjacent one. Several interesting observations have been made as to the changeableness of the vegetation from year to year at one and the same locality.

On account of the considerable expenses caused by a travel to and a stay of some months in Finmarken, especially East-Finmarken, it has been necessary to limit the dredging so as to get only a passable survey of the vegetation in the sublitoral and elitoral regions. Farther I have as a rule dredged by myself, but that is, of course, much troublesome and often also waste of time, particularly along the open coast with a heavy setting of the current. A more thorough sifting of at least the sublitoral zone would, no doubt, bring to light many interesting forms and give a better general view of the biology of the marine Flora in this part of the arctic region. However, dredging is difficult or almost impossible in localities where *Alariæ* and *Laminariæ* clothe the bottom in greater abundance, and that is the case almost everywhere along the rocky and exposed part of the coast. They form here large submarine «woods» composed principally of *Laminaria hyperborea*, *L. digitata* and *Alariæ*, 6—12 feet high with thick and vigorous stems, or *L. saccharina* with a lamina of 10 feet or more in length.

Here the dredge hardly will be able to sound. But just in such places a large number of smaller algæ form a luxuriant «underwood». I have mostly used other instruments than the common dredge but not always with good luck.

In zoography East- and West-Finmarken are regarded as two distinct provinces within the arctic region. Cp. Sars in Tromsö Mus. Aarsh. II, p. 62. In an algological point of view there is, certainly, not so great a difference that they may be regarded as really distinct. But still there is, in some respects, a rather great difference. The algæ that characterize the marine Flora at East-Finmarken are also at West-Finmarken forming the main mass of the vegetation. But the subordinate elements and the composition of the formations are often different. West-Finmarken forms the northern limit to a number of boreal forms, either wanting at East-Finmarken, or appearing here in scattered and more or less dwarfish individuals. And at East-Finmarken also occur several high-northern algæ, not found, as far as hitherto known, in other parts of the Norwegian Polar Sea. Farther, many algæ which are, as far as known, exclusively litoral in the southern part of the Norwegian Polar Sea, or even at West-Finmarken, descend sometimes pretty far in the sublitoral zone. And others appear generally in the limit between the litoral and sublitoral region, or at extreme low-water mark, but on the other hand, more south they are living higher up. It is also worth noticing that the reproductive organs often seem to be developed later in the year than farther south. A more detailed view as to the composition of the Flora in general and its relation to other parts of the Polar Sea will be given in connection with a List of the marine Algæ of West-Finmarken, which I hope to be able to publish before long.

It may be remarked that, with regard to the extend of the district, I have followed the political limits, referring to

East-Finmarken the tract from Sværholt eastward to Jakobselv. In zoography the tract from North Cape to Sværholt is usually also referred to East-Finmarken, but I know as yet but a little of this tract. However that is by a comparison of the marine Flora a thing of minor importance.

Tromsö 28. XI. 1889.

Ser. **Florideæ** (Lamour.) Thur.
in Le Jol. Liste Alg. Cherb. p. 16; Lamour. Essai p. 115; lim. mut.

Fam. **Corallinaceæ** (Lamour.) Hauck
Meeresalg. p. 19; Lamour. Hist. Polyp. p. 244.

Gen. **Corallina** (Tourn.) Lamour.
Hist. Polyp. p. 245; Tourn. Inst. Herb. p. 570; char. mut.

Corallina officinalis L.
Fauna Suec. p. 539.

f. typica.
Descr. Corallina officinalis Aresch. in J. G. Ag. Spec. Alg. 2, p. 562.
Fig.   „   „   Harv. Phyc. Brit. t. 222.
Exsicc. „   „   Aresch. Alg. Scand. exsicc. Nr. 8.

f. *flexilis* Kjellm.
N. Ish. Algfl. p. 114.
Descr. Corallina officinalis f. flexilis Kjellm. l. c.

f. *robusta* Kjellm.
l. c.
Descr. Corallina officinalis f. robusta Kjellm. l. c.

The most common form of this species is f. *typica*, but f. *flexilis* is also pretty common on several places. I have not met with typical specimens of f. *robusta*, I found however at Berlevåg an intermediate form between it and f. *typica*.

The species is generally litoral and occurs chiefly in rock-pools in the upper part of the zone, or on rocks and stones at low-water mark. From the sublitoral zone I have seen a few specimens, fastened to roots of *Laminaria*, which were cast on shore. It occurs on exposed coasts as well as in sheltered places. Specimens collected in June, July and the earlier half of August were sterile.

Distribution; Pretty common along the whole coast but mostly in small numbers.

Gen. **Lithothamnion** Phil.

Wiegm. Arch. 1, p. 387.

Lithothamnion soriferum Kjellm.
N. Ish. Algfl. p. 117.
Descr. Lithothamnion soriferum Kjellm l. c.
Fig.   „   „   Kjellm. l. c. t. 1.

This species approaches on one side to *L. alcicorne* and on the other side it not seldom assumes a form, in general appearance very much like *L. norvegicum*.

The plant is sublitoral and occurs usually on a depth of 10—15 fathoms, on open as well as sheltered coasts, but it appears to prefer protected places and it enters to the end of the deeper bays. It grows on sandy and shingly or clay-mingled bottom. I have taken specimens with tetraspores in June and August.

Distribution. It seems to be pretty common everywhere, and at some places, for inst. Lebesby, abundant. I have taken it at Lebesby, Kjöllefjord, Mehavn, Vardö and at Kirkenæs in Sydvaranger.

Lithothamnion norvegicum Aresch. (Kjellm.)
N. Ish. Algfl. p. 122; Lithothamnion calcareum var. **norvegicum** Aresch. Obs. Phyc. 3, p. 4.
Descr. Lithothamnion calcareum var. norvegicum Aresch. l. c. p. 4—5.
Fig.   „   norvegicum Kjellm. N. Ish. Algfl. t. 5, fig. 9—10.

I have only met with some few barren specimens of this species. As mentioned before, it seems to be nearly related to the preceding one, and I should be inclined to consider it a form of that species. However, it is a plant little known, as only sterile specimens have been found. It grows on similar localities as *L. soriferum.*

Distribution: Only found at Mehavn, very rare.

Lithothamnion intermedium Kjellm.
N. Ish. Algfl. p. 127.
Descr. Lithothamnion intermedium Kjellm. 1. c.
Fig.   „   „   „   l. c. t. 4.

Sublitoral, growing on various bottom on a depth of 3—15 fathoms water. Most frequently I met it on sandy or clayish bottom on exposed coasts as well as rather sheltered ones. It occurs mostly in thinly scattered individuals, never, as far as I know, in considerable numbers. Tetraspore-specimens have been collected in July and August.

Distribution: The species seems to occure everywhere along the coast. I have taken it at Lebesby, Mehavn, Havningberg and Vardö, but scarce; Vadsö, pretty plentiful; Kjelmö, rather scarce.

Lithothamnion glaciale Kjellm.
N. Ish. Algfl. p. 123.
Descr. Lithothamnion glaciale Kjellm. 1. c.
Fig.   „   „   „   l. c. t. 2—3.

This species is, in the Polar Sea, one of the largest of the genus. I have seen specimens which had a diameter of about 0.5 m. It is sublitoral and occurs on various depths, though usually on a depth of 10—15 fathoms. But I have also met with large and well developed specimens on a depth of only 3—5 fathoms. It prefers sandy and shingly bottom and is most often met with on sheltered places. Tetraspore-specimens have been taken in June, July and August.

Distribution: Found at Kjelmö, pretty plentiful but local; Mehavn and Kjöllefjord, scarce; and at Lebesby, local but abundant.

Lithothamnion Ungeri Kjellm.

N. Ish. Algfl. p. 120.

Descr. Lithothamnion byssoides Unger, Leithakalk p. 19—20, sec. Kjellm. l. c.

Fig.   „   „   Unger l. c. t. 5, fig. 1—8.

I have not seen Unger's description of this species but by comparison of specimens from Tromsö, determined by Kjellman, it also occurs at East-Finmarken. Here it sometimes attains a considerable size. I have taken specimens, which were about 22 cm. long, 18 cm. broad and 9 cm. high. However, it seems to be rather much varying as to form and ramification. All the specimens collected at East-Finmarken belong to the typical form, but from Malangen and other places in Tromsö amt I have specimens which are somewhat differing. They will be described by a later occasion.

The species is always sublitoral and oftenest occurs on sandy and shingly bottom within the upper part of the zone, on a depth of 3—10 fathoms water. It thrives best on sheltered places and is seldom met with on open shore. At East-Finmarken I have taken tetraspore-specimens in the beginning of August, in Tromsö amt in June.

Distribution: Found at Kjelmö in Sydvaranger, pretty plentiful but local, Vardö and Havningberg, scarce.

Lithothamnion flavescens Kjellm.

N. Ish. Algfl. p. 129.

Descr. Lithothamnion flavescens Kjellm. l. c.

Fig.   „   „   „   l. c. t. 6, fig. 1—7.

A few specimens of this alga I found attached to *L. glaciale* within the sublitoral zone on a depth of 4—6 fathoms, and to stones and shells of Balanidæ on a depth of 10—15 fathoms water. It bears tetraspores in July.

Distribution: Found at Kjelmö and Kirkenæs in Sydvaranger, rare.

Lithothamnion circumscriptum Strömf.
Isl. Algveg. p. 20.
Descr. Lithothamnion circumscriptum Strömf. l. c.
Fig. „ „ „ l. c. t. 1, fig. 4—8.

Of this plant, before only found at Iceland, I met with a few specimens in rock-pools between tides, fastened to shells, and within the sublitoral zone, on a depth of 5—10 fathoms, fastened to stones. Tetraspore-specimens have been collected at the end of July.

Distribution: Found at Mehavn and at Kjelmö in Sydvaranger, rare. Probably it is more commonly spread.

Lithothamnion polymorphum (L.) Aresch.
in J. G. Ag. Spec. Alg. 2, p 524; Millepora polymorpha L. Syst. Nat. p. 1285; ex parte.
Descr. Lithothamnion polymorphum Strömf. Isl. Algveg. p. 19.
Fig „ „ Hauck, Meeresalg. t 1, fig. 4
Exsicc. „ „ Aresch. Alg. Scand. exsicc. Nr. 302.

Litoral and sublitoral. In the litoral zone it most commonly occurs in rock-pools, and in the sublitoral zone chiefly on a depth of 3—5 fathoms, but it also descends to a depth of 10 fathoms water. It sometimes grows gregarious, covering rather large spaces of the bottom, and often serves as a substratum for *Alariæ* but especially smaller algæ. I have taken tetraspore-specimens in the beginning of August.

Distribution: Pretty common all along the shore, at some places rather abundant.

Gen. **Lithophyllum** (Phil.) Rosan.
Melob. p. 79; Phil. Wiegm. Arch. 1, p. 385; lim. mut.

Lithophyllum Lenormandi (Aresch.) Rosan.
l. c. p. 85; Melobesia Lenormandi Aresch. in J. G. Ag. Spec. Alg. 2, p. 514.
Descr. Lithophyllum Lenormandi Rosan. l. c. p. 85
Fig. „ „ „ l. c. t 5, fig. 16—17 ; t. 6, fig. 1—3.

Fig. Lithophyllum Lenormandi Hauck, Meeresalg. t. 3, fig. 4.
Exsicc. Melobesia „ Hohenack. Alg. Mar. Nr. 296.

This species is litoral as well as sublitoral. In the litoral zone it grows in rock-pools, on rocks or attached to shells (chiefly *Mytilus*) in the lower part of the zone. In the sublitoral zone it descends to a depth of 10 fathoms and principally covers smaller stones[1]. It is most abundantly met with on a depth of 1—3 fathoms and at some places (for inst. Kjöllefjord) growing in as considerable numbers as to give the vegetation its character. It occurs as well on exposed places as on sheltered ones. I have taken tetraspore-specimens at the end of June, in July and in the beginning of August.

Distribution: Pretty common almost everywhere, at some places abundant.

Lithophyllum læve Strömf.
Isl. Algveg. p. 21.

Descr. Lithophyllum læve Strömf. l. c.
Fig. „ „ „ l. c. t. 1, fig. 11—12.

I have met with a few certain specimens of this plant, which till now has been found only at Iceland. The species approaches very nearly to the preceding one, as the author remarks himself. To me it seems doubtful whether it can be specifically distinguished from the former. The plant grows on similar localities as *L. Lenormandi.* Tetraspore-specimens have been collected in July.

Distribution: Found at Mehavn and at Kirkenæs in Sydvaranger. Perhaps it is more commonly distributed and some of my notes on *L. Lenormandi* really refer to *L. læve.*

Lithophyllum zonatum nob.

In the most eastern part of the district I found a so-

---

[1]. Perhaps it descends to a still greater depth. In Tromsö amt it is sublitoral as well as elitoral, descending to a depth of about 30 fathoms.

litary specimen of an alga, which I suppose belongs to the genus *Lithophyllum*, and not referrible to any known species of the genus. Although it is a rather doubtful one, and the specimen is young and barren, I want to give it a name. It grew fastened to *Lithothamnion glaciale*, and it very much reminds of young specimens of *Lithophyllum arcticum* Kjellm. Cp. Kariska Hafvets algv. p. 16, t. 1, fig. 1. But according to Kjellman, who has had the kindness to examine it, it cannot be referred to that species. It differs by its thicker crust, being unbranched, and by wanting ridges.

The plant forms incrustations on the host plant. The crust is rather closely adherent to the substratum, 0.75—1.5 mm. thick, and the surface uneven. The uneveness seems to be caused by the substratum, to which it clings, though not always closely. The circumference is not everywhere free; the free part is 0.5—1 mm. thick, and the margin shallowly lobated and somewhat undulated, with distinct subconcentric stripes or feeble ridges.

The specimen was found in the harbour of Kjelmö in Sydvaranger, on a depth of about 3—4 fathoms.

Gen. **Melobesia** (Lamour.) Rosan.
Melob. p 53; Lamour. Bull. soc. Phil. 1812, sec. Rosan. l. c. p. 60.

Melobesia macrocarpa Rosan.
Melob. p. 74.
Descr. Melobesia macrocarpa Rosan l. c.
Fig. „ „ „ l. c. t. 4, fig. 2—8 et 11—20.

In the upper part of the sublitoral zone at Kiberg in the neighbourhood of Vardö I found a couple of specimens of a coarse *Melobesia*, fastened to the stipe of *Laminaria hyperborea*, which resembles this species. However, they were sterile and, therefore, the determination is not quite sure,

But only this species has been found on the mentioned host plant in Nordland and at Iceland.

Distribution: Only found at Kiberg in Varanger, very rare.

Fam. **Rhodomelaceæ** J. G. Ag.
Symb. p. 23; Spec. Alg. 2, p. 787.

Gen. **Odonthalia** Lyngb.
Hydr. Dan. p. 9.

Odonthalia dentata (L.) Lyngb.
l. c. Fucus dentatus L. Mant p. 35.
Descr. Odonthalia dentata J. G. Ag. Spec. Alg. 2, p. 899.
Fig. „ „ Harv. Phyc. Brit. t. 34.
Exsicc. „ „ Alg. Scand. exsicc. Nr. 56.
   Syn. Fucus dentatus Gunn. Fl Norv. 2, p. 91.
   „ pinnatifidus Gunn. l. c. p. 104.

Also at East-Finmarken occur two forms of this species, one with broader, the other with narrower frond, f. *angusta* Harv., but as stated by Kjellman they run so gradually into each other that no limit can be drawn between them. The former occosionally grows on open shore and the latter in the interior of deeper bays, or on sheltered places. At Kirkenæs in Sydvaranger I met with a form which had a thread-narrow frond, but also this seems to run into the narrow one mentioned above, and may be regarded only as a local variety. As well known, several pelagic algæ get a form more or less differing when they enter into deep bays or grow on much sheltered localities.

The species in question is sublitoral and occurs on a depth of 3—20 fathoms, on various bottom. It seems to be best developed on stony, shelly or gravelly bottom on a depth of 6—12 fathoms, and then commonly growing together with *Delesseria* and *Ptilota*. All the specimens I have collected myself in the summer have been sterile. However Kjellman has at West-Finmarken, at the end of August, met with specimens with the beginnings of sporocarps. At Lödingen in Nordland I have found specimens with tetraspores in December and with sporocarps in February.

Distribution: Commonly spread along the whole coast, never in considerable numbers, and enters almost to the end of the greater bays.

Gen. **Rhodomela** (Ag.) J. G. Ag.

Spec. Alg. 2, p. 874; Ag. Spec. Alg. 1, p. 368; ex parte.

Rhodomela lycopodioides (L.) Ag.

l. c. p. 377; Fucus lycopodioides L. Syst. Nat. 2, p. 717.

f. *typica*.

α *compacta* Kjellm.

N. Ish. Algfl. p. 139.

Descr. Rhodomela lycopodioides J. G. Ag. Spec. Alg. 2, p. 885.
Fig. „ „ Harv. Phyc. Brit. t. 50.
Exsicc. „ „ Aresch. Alg. Scand. exsicc. Nr. 3.

β *laxa* Kjellm.

l. c. p. 140.

Descr. Rhodomela lycopodioides f. typica β laxa Kjellm. l. c.
Fig. „ „ „ „ „ l. c. t. 9, fig 1.

γ *tenera* Kjellm.

l. c. p. 140.

Descr. Rhodomela lycopodioides f. typica γ tenera Kjellm. l. c.
Fig. „ „ „ „ „ l. c. t. 9, fig 2.

f. *cladostephus* J. G. Ag. (Kjellm.)

Spetsb. Thall. 1, p. 8; Rhodomela cladostephus J. G. Ag. Spetsb. Alg. Till. p. 48.

α *densa* Kjellm.

l. c. p. 140.

Descr. Aphanarthron cladostephus J. G. Ag. Spetsb. Alg. Bidr. p. 8—9.
Fig.   "   "   "   Spetsb. Alg. t. 2.

 f. *flagellaris* Kjellm.

 l. c. p. 141.
Descr. Rhodomela lycopodioides f. flagellaris Kjellm. l. c.
Fig.   "   "   "   "   t. 10, fig. 1—2.

 Syn. Fucus lycopodioides Gunn. Fl. Norv. 2, p. 80.
  "   "   Wg. Fl. Lapp. p. 505.
  "   subfuscus Wg. l. c.
  Conferva squarrosa Gunn. l. c. p. 105.
  Gigartina lycopodioides Lyngb. Hydr. Dan. p. 45.
  "   subfusca Sommerf. in Act. Nidros. p. 51.

  This species is one of the most common of the Florideæ of East-Finmarken, and here too somewhat varying. It appears as a rule under the form above mentioned, named by Kjellman f. *typica* α *compacta*. I have only some few times met with the forms β *laxa* and γ *tenera*, the former at Mehavn and Omgang, in rock-pools between tides, and washed ashore, probably from the uppermost part of the sublitoral zone, and the latter only at Mehavn, in rock-pools between tides. Of the form *cladostephus*, new to the Flora of Norway, I found a solitary specimen washed ashore at Mehavn. It belongs to the subform *densa*, is about 10 cm. long, and fully corresponds with the description and figures given by Agardh. But, on the other hand, it is nearly allied to f. *typica* α *compacta*. The colour is somewhat paler, and it retains its colour in drying better than the named form. Two small specimens of a *Rhodomela* which I also found at Mehavn, in a rock-pool at low-water mark, I have referred to f. *flagellaris*, formerly only known from Spitzbergen. They are about 3 cm. long and do not fully correspond with that form but seem to be a transition between it and f. *setacea*, although most nearly related to the former. I possess typical specimens of f. *flagellaris* from Lödingen in Nordland taken on several fathoms water.

Rh. lycopodioides f. typica α compacta is properly a litoral form, and occurs most commonly in the lowest part of this zone, but at several places it also appears abundant a few feet below extreme low-water mark. In scattered individuals I have met with it as far down as about 10 fathoms. Best developed and most abundant it grows on somewhat steep rocks on open coast, and in rock-pools between tides on exposed places. It also is met with in rather sheltered coves and in somewhat enclosed bays and sounds, but not in the inner of the deeper fjords.

The species grows commonly 10—15 cm. long, but rather often specimens are met with, which have a length of 20—25 cm. It probably develops reproductive organs all the summer, but not richly (perhaps also in winter). I have taken specimens with sporocarps and antheridia in June and July, at West Finmarken in May and June, and at Nordland in the middle of February; tetraspores in June and July, at West-Finmarken besides that in May and September, and at Nordland in January.

Distribution: Common and abundant almost everywhere along the shore, as a rule wanting or at least scarce in the inner part of the deeper bays.

Gen. **Polysiphonia** Grev.
Fl. Edinb. p. 308, sec. J. G. Ag. Spec. Alg. 2, p. 900.

Polysiphonia urceolata (Lightf.) Grev.
Fl. Edinb. p. 309; Conferva urceolata Lightf. in Dillw. Intr. p. 82.

f. *typica.*
Descr Polysiphonia urceolata α urceolata J. G. Ag. Spec. Alg. 2, p. 970.
Fig.   „   „   Harv. Phyc. Brit. t. 167.
Exsicc.   „   „   Aresch. Alg. Scand. exsicc. Nr. 68.
           „   „   Wyatt, Alg. Danm. Nr. 133.

f. *patens* (Dillw.) J. G. Ag.
l. c. p. 971; Conferva patens Dillw. Syn. p. 83.

α *distans* nob.

Descr. Polysiphonia urceolata β patens J. G. Ag. l. c.
Fig. Conferva patens Dillw. l. c. t. G.
Exsicc. Polysiphonia patens Crouan, Alg. Finist. Nr. 289.

β *fasciculata* nob.
f. ramulis ultimis in fasciculos densissimos congestis.

f. *formosa* Suhr (J. G. Ag.)

l. c. p. 971; Polysiphonia formosa Suhr, in Bot. Zeit. 1831, p. 709, sec. J. G. Ag. l. c.
Descr. Polysiphonia urceolata γ formosa J. G. Ag. l. c.
Fig. Hutchinsia urceolata Lyngb. Hydr. Dan. t. 34.
Exsicc. Cfr. Polysiphonia patens Aresch. Alg. Scand. exsicc. Ser. 1, Nr. 58.

f. *comosa* Ag. (J. G. Ag.)

l. c. p. 971; Hutchinsia comosa Ag. Spec. Alg. p. 72.
Descr Polysiphonia urceolata δ comosa J. G. Ag. l. c.
Fig. Conferva stricta Dillw. Syn. t. 40.

f. *roseola* Ag. (J. G. Ag.)

l. c. p. 971; Hutchinsia roseola Ag. Spec. Alg. p. 92.
Descr. Polysiphonia urceolata ε roseola J. G. Ag. l. c.
Fig.   „   formosa Harv. Phyc. Brit. t. 168.
Exsicc.   „   roseola Aresch. Alg. Scand. exsicc. Ser. 1, Nr. 59;
                              Ser. 2, Nr. 69.
              „   formosa Wyatt, Alg. Danm. Nr. 216.

Syn. Conferva stricta Wg. Fl. Lapp. p. 512.

The species is also along the coast of the northern Norway somewhat variable with reference to the habit, and, moreover, it here often becomes coarser and more rigid than more south. Thus the Finmarkian specimens of f. *typica* are usually rather coarser and more robust than for inst. Swedish and English ones. Cp. A r e s c h., Alg. Scand. exsicc. Nr. 68 and W y a t t, Alg. Danm. Nr. 133.

The form named by me f. *patens* β *fasciculata* is coarser and still more rigid than any form of f. *typica*, and the secondary branches are remarkably squarrose or recurvated, in which respects it is, as far as I can judge, nearly related to *f. patens*. It differs, however, by the outermost branches forming rather dense corymb clusters, whose secondary branches are short and somewhat robust, hooked backwards or angular, closely compact and often connected with one another by peculiar fastening organs. I suppose it to be the same form mentioned by Kjellman from Nordland in N. Ish. Algfl. p. 153, and besides that it has also been found at Haugesund. At East-Finmarken it occurred on an iron buoy, which had been laid out in August, 1885, and was put on shore for cleaning in the summer 1887. The specimens had a length of 9—14 cm. and were richly sporocarp-bearing in the middle of July. Some of them are more nearly related to α *distans* than to β *fasciculata*. On the other hand, this form reminds of *f. typica* and sometimes approaches it nearly by its branches being more or less erect.

The other forms above citied also occur at Finmarken, but by no means distinctly marked out. I have certainly met with specimens which almost fully coincide with *Polysiphonia patens* Aresch. Alg. Scand. exsicc. Ser. 1, No. 58, which, according to J. G. Agardh is identic with f. *formosa*, but I consider merely an intermediate form between f. *typica* and f. *formosa*, resembling the former by its more or less erect (or sometimes patent, not recurvated) branches, and the latter by its flaccidity. The most characteristic of these forms at East-Finmarken is f. *roseola*, which, however, is more densely branched, somewhat coarser, more flaccid and the lateral branches more erect than the above quoted specimens distributed by Areschoug and Wyatt. It closely resembles the habit-figure in Harvey's Phyc. Brit. t. 168. I have referred to f. *comosa* some specimens, which resemble f. *roseola* except that they are rather rigid and straight in the lower part of the frond. The forms are very variable with reference to the length of the cells.

The present species is litoral as well as sublitoral. Best

developed it appears on rocks at low-water mark on exposed places, more seldom in rock-pools between tides, and it grows often gregarious in rather considerable masses. In the sublitoral zone, to the lowest limit of which it sometimes descend, it occurs more scattered. Here it always prefers solid rocky bottom, sometimes also it is found on looser or even on clayish bottom, but at such places it assumes loosely entangled and sparingly branched tufts. It is usually met with on a depth of 3—10 fathoms in company with *Ptilota*, *Delesseria* and *Rhodophyllis*, or epiphytic especially on the first one. Often it almost covers *Ptilota pectinata* forming rather bristly and sparingly branched threads, or loosely entangled tufts. It also often grows in large numbers on the stems of *Alaria* or more commonly *Laminaria hyperborea* within the upper part of the sublitoral zone. The plant has generally a length of 8—15 cm., but not rarely it becomes 20 cm. long. It bears tetraspores in the later half of June, in July and August; sporocarps in July and, more richly, August.

Distribution: Common and mostly abundant along the open shore, but it also enters almost to the end of the great bays. The form *patens* has only been found at Berlevåg; f. *formosa* at Vardö and Sværholt; f. *comosa* at Syltefjord and Sværholt; and f. *roseola* at Sværholt.

Polysiphonia fastigiata (Roth.) Grev.

Fl. Edinb. p. 308; Ceramium fastigiatum Roth, Fl. Germ. 3, p. 463.
Descr. Polysiphonia fastigiata J. G. Ag. Spec Alg. 2, p. 1029.
Fig. "   "   Harv. Phyc. Brit. t. 299.
Exsicc. "   "   Aresch. Alg. Scand. exsicc. No. 4.
  Syn. Conferva omissa Gunn. Fl. Norv. 2, p. 78.
    "   polymorpha Gunn. l. c. p. 92.
    "   "   Wg. Fl. Lapp. p. 511.
   Hutchinsia fastigiata Sommerf. in Act. Nidros p. 51.

The species is litoral and occurs at East-Finmarken only on the same host plant as elsewhere, *Ozothallia nodosa*. All the specimens I have examined in June and July were sterile. But in the earlier half of August individuals with young tetraspores were pretty common at Vardö and Pasvig. It has been found with reproductive organs at West-Finmarken in July, August, September, October, and in Tromsö amt from June to November, most richly in September. Thus it might seem that this alga here develops its reproductive organs somewhat later in the year than at West-Finmarken and farther to the south.

Distribution: Pretty common everywhere along the open coast. It does not enter as far into the great bays as the host plant. Yet it occurs even at Lebesby in Laksefjord in rather large numbers. The plant seems to decrease in number of individuals to the east. Although it appears abundant on some localities even as far east as at Pasvig, still it is less commonly distributed in the eastern than in the western part of the district.

Polysiphonia arctica J. G. Ag.
Spec. Alg. 2, p. 1034.
Descr. Polysiphonia arctica J. G. Ag. l. c.
         „   „ Gobi, Algenfl. Weiss. Meer. p. 26.
Exsicc.   „   „ Aresch. Alg. Scand. exsicc. No. 403.

This plant is always sublitoral. I do not know far it descends. On the places I met with it, it grew on a depth of 3—10 fathoms, sometimes fastened to stones or shells of Balanidæ, sometimes to other algæ, as *Laminaria*-roots and *Lithothamnia*. It prefers stony or shingly bottom and grows often together with *Dichloria*, generally in scattered individuals.

The plant seems here to be coarser than for inst. at Spitzbergen, judging from a few specimens I have seen from there. The size is most commonly 8—15 cm., but I have met with specimens which were even 30 cm. long. The pericentrale siphons are generally 6 in number, rarely 7, but often only 5 even in the elder parts of the frond. A similar relation hos Gobi observed on specimens from the White Sea and from Novaya Zemlya. Cp. Gobi, Algenfl. Weiss. Meer. p. 27. All the specimens examined by me at the end of June, in the beginning of July and August were sterile.

Distribution: Probably commonly spread all along the open coast. I have taken specimens at Koskjælhavn, Mehavn, Vadsö and at Kjelmö in Sydvaranger.

Polysiphonia nigrescens (Huds.) Harv.
Br. Fl. 2, p. 332; Conferva nigrescens Huds. Engl. Bot. t. 1717.

f. *pectinata* Ag.
Hutchinsia nigrescens β pectinata Ag. Syst. Alg. p. 151.
Descr. Polysiphonia nigrescens α pectinata J. G. Ag. Spec. Alg. 2, p. 1058.
Fig. Conferva nigrescens Engl. Bot. t. 1717.
Exsicc. Polysiphonia Brodiæi Aresch. Alg. Scand. exsicc. Ser. 1, No. 57.
    „   „ Aresch. Alg. Scand. exsicc. No. 63 et 152;
    „ nigrescens Aresch. l. c. No. 62 et 304.
Syn. Conferva atrorubens Wg. Fl. Lapp. p. 511.
    Rhodomela gracilis Kleen, Nordl. Alg. p. 12.
    Polysiphonia nigrescens Kleen l. c. p. 13.

At East-Finmarken I have only met with this species in the lower part of the litoral zone, on stones or attached to *Fucus vesiculosus* and *Rhodymenia palmata*. Here it appears to prefer sheltered places, I at least have only seen it in the inner part of deep bays. The specimens were small, only 6—10 cm. long. In July it was steril. At West-Finmarken I have taken it with sporocarps in the middle of August.

Distribution: Only found at Kirkenæs in Sydvaranger and at Nyborg, at the end of Varangerfjord, where it was pretty plentiful but local.

Fam. **Spongiocarpeæ** Grev.
Alg. Brit. p. 68.

Gen. Polyides Ag.
Spec. Alg. 1, p. 390.

Polyides rotundus (Gmel.) Grev.
Alg. Brit. p. 70; Fucus rotundus Gmel. Hist. Fuc. p. 110.
Descr. Polyides lumbricalis J. G. Ag. Spec. Alg. 2, p. 721.
Fig. Polyides rotundus Harv. Phyc. Brit. t. 95.
Exsicc. „ „ Aresch. Alg. Scand. exsicc. No. 252.

    Syn Fucus caprinus Gunn. Fl. Norv. 1, p. 96 et in Act Nidros. p. 82.
    Furcellaria rotunda Sommerf. in Act. Nidros. p. 51.

This alga is chiefly litoral, growing on rocks at low-water mark, or in rock-pools, but it also occurs in the upper part of the sublitoral zone, on a depth of about 4 fathoms. The specimens are small and often rather slender, but still they approach most nearly the typical form. I have taken specimens bearing tetraspores at the end of June.

Distribution: Scattered and scarce along the open shore, and not met with in the inner part of the great fjords.

Fam. **Delesseriaceæ** J. G. Ag.
Epicr. p. 444. Cfr. Alg. med. p. 155.

Gen. **Delesseria** (Lamour.) J. G. Ag.
Epicr. p. 477; Lamour. Ess. p. 122; ex parte.

Delesseria alata (Huds.) Lamour.
Ess. p. 124; Fucus alatus Huds. Fl. Angl. p. 578.
Descr. Delesseria alata J. G. Ag. Epicr. p. 483.
Fig. „ „ Harv. Phyc. Brit. t. 247.
Exsicc. „ „ Aresch. Alg. Scand. exsicc. No. 75.

    Syn. Delesseria alata Kleen, Nordl. Alg. p. 14.
    „ „ var. augustissima Kleen l. c.?
    „ angustissima Kjellm. Ish Algfl. p. 172?
    Fucus alatus Gunn. Fl. Norv. 2, p. 91.
    „ „ Wg. Wg. Fl. Lapp. p. 492.

The most common form of the species resembles fig. 2, t. 247 in. Harv. Phyc. Brit. and usually becomes 3—5 cm. high, not exceeding 10 cm., by 1—2 mm. in breadth.[1])

As far as I have seen the plant only occurs in the litoral zone, either in rock pools or more frequently on steep rocks covered by *Fucus* and *Ozothallia*, and on the walls of grotto-shaped cavities together with *Ptilota elegans*. It is only to be found on open coasts and appears best developed in much exposed localities. All the specimens collected in June, July and August were sterile.

Distribution: The plant occurs all along the unsheltered coast, and at several places, for inst. Mehavn, Berlevåg, Havningberg and Vardö, it is pretty common but not plentiful.

Delesseria sinuosa (Good. et Woodw.) Lamour.
Ess. p. 124; Fucus sinuosus Good. et Woodw. Linn. Trans. 3, p. 111.

f. *typica*.
Descr. Delesseria sinuosa J. G. Ag. Spec. Alg. 2, p. 691.
Fig.   „   „   Harv. Phyc. Brit. t. 259.
Exsicc. „   „   Wyatt. Alg. Danm. No. 62.

f. *quercifolia* Turn.
Hist. Fuc. 1, p. 74.

---

[1].) Kleen says (l. c.): „When it *(Delesseria alata)* occurs on dark places between tides it seems to assume the var. *angustisima* (Harv. Phyc. Brit. t. 83). This form was common on stones beneath *Fucaceæ*". Taking this for granted Kjollman records *D. angustissima* in his Ish. Algfl. (p. 172). Of course I should not deny or even think it unlikely that *D. angustissima* is to be found in Nordland, but, on the other hand, I want to point out the fact that the narrow form of *D. alata* also there is common just on localities like those quoted by Kleen for *D. angustissima*. Moreover he says that *D. alata* grows in rock-pools between tides (and within the sublitoral zone), but he adds nothing about its occurrence in other parts of the litoral zone. I therefore suppose it to be highly probable that Kleens *D. alata* var. *angustissima* belongs to the narrow form of *D. alata*,

Descr. Fucus sinuosus γ quercifolius Turn, l. c.
Exsicc. Delesseria sinuosa Aresch. Alg. Scand. exsicc. No. 74.

   f. *lingulata* Ag.
      Spec. Alg. 1, p. 175.
Descr. Delesseria sinuosa γ lingulata Ag. l. c.
Fig. Phycodrys sinuosa Kütz. Tab. Phyc. 16, t. 20, fig. e—f.
   Syn. Fucus roseus Fl. Dan. t. 652.
      „   sinuosus Wg. Fl. Lapp. p. 491.

This is properly a pelagic species, and appears along the unsheltered coast almost ever in the typical form, or forms which are most nearly related to this. But it also enters into the bays or occurs on sheltered places, yet here it does not develop to the same luxuriancy as on open shore and assumes more or less differing forms. It is at least on such places the most extreme forms are observed. Thus f. *lingulata* is only to be met with in more or less sheltered localities, or on a greater depth, and generally on looser bottom than the other forms. Of the form *quercifolia* I have only seen a couple of specimens at East-Finmarken, or properly a transition between this form and f. *typica*, but most likely to be reckoned to the former.

The present species is litoral, sublitoral as well as elitoral. Within the litoral region it is not often met with, and only in rock-pools, generally attached to *Laminaria*-roots. The sublitoral zone is its proper native place. On open shore and rocky bottom, on a depth of 5—15 fathoms the best developed and most luxuriant individuals are collected, attaining a length of 40 cm. Large and well developed specimens are also to be found growing on the stems and root of *Laminaria hyperborea*. I only know little of its occurrence in the elitoral zone, as I have here only two times met with a few living but somewhat stunted individuals, on a depth of about 25 fathoms. Yet this has been on loose and clayish bottom where the plant seldom thrives, and on such localities it usually assumes forms more or less differing from the typical one. The proper time for the development of reproductive organs at East-Finmarken seems not to be the summer months. In July and August I have taken a few specimens with sporocarps and in the same months others with tetraspores. At Nordland it has been found with sporocarps in great numbers in March and tetraspores in February, but never in the summer months.

Distribution: Common and rather plentiful all along the coast, rather scarce in the inner part of the bays.

Fam. **Rhodymeniaceæ** (Harv.) J. G. Ag.
Epicr. p. 307; Harv. Phyc. Brit. Syn. p. VIII; lim. mut.

Gen. **Hydrolapathum** (Stackh.) J. G. Ag.
Epicr. p. 369; Stackh. Tentamen. sec. Alg. Och. p. 247; char. mut.

Hydrolapathum sanguineum (L.) Stackh.
l. c. Fucus sanguineus L. Mant. p. 136.
Descr. Hydrolapathum sanguineum J. G. Ag. l. c. p. 370.
Fig. Delesseria sanguinea Harv. Phyc. Brit. t. 151.
Exsicc. „   „   Aresch. Alg. Scand. exsicc. No. 73.
Syn. Fucus sanguineus Gunn. Fl. Norv. 2, p. 91.
„   „   Wg. Fl. Lapp. p. 491.
Wormskioldia sanguinea Kleen. Nordl. Alg. p. 16.

It was quite unexpected to meet with large and very luxuriant individuals of this species in the eastern part of the district. Two times (in 1887 and 1889) I found washed ashore at Vardö and attached to the stem of *Laminaria hyperborea* a few specimens, one of which was about 70 cm. long, with the leaf-shaped branches reaching 28 cm. in length by 4—9 cm. in breadth. The specimens were quite fresh, the host plant likewise, and cast on shore after a heavy gale the night before I found it. (The locality was investigated the day before). I therefore cannot suppose it to have been carried thither from any other territory. Moreover I have taken a small specimen at Svärholt fastened to *Ptilota plumosa*, on a depth of about 5 fathoms. It is unknown to me when it develops its reproductive organs here. At Nordland I have collected tetrasporiferous specimens with contemporary almost fully developed thallom in the middle of May.

Distribution: Not precisely known to me. Only found at Vardö, washed ashore, scarce; and at Svärholt, a single specimen.

Gen. Rhodophyllis Kütz.
Bot. Zeit. 1847, p. 23.

Rhodophyllis dichotoma (Lepech.) Gobi
Algenfl. Weiss. Meer. p. 35; Fucus dichotomus Lepech. Comment. Petrop. p. 479, t. 22, sec. Gobi l. c.
Descr. Rhodophyllis veprecula J. G. Ag. Epicr. p. 362.
Fig. „ „ Kütz. Tab. Phyc. 19, t. 52.
 „ dichotoma Kjellm. N. Ish. Algfl. t. 12, fig. 3.
Exsicc. „ veprecula Aresch. Alg. Scand exsicc. No. 404.
Syn. Calliblepharis ciliata Kleen, Nordl. Alg. p. 14.
Fucus ciliatus Gunn. Fl. Norv. 2, p. 96.
 „ laciniatus Gunn. l. c. p. 143.
 „ pumilus Fl. Dan t. 1066.
Chondrus crispus ε pumilus Lyngb. Hydr. Dan. p. 16.

A sublitoral alga, most frequent and best developed on stony or shingly bottom within the upper part of the zone, on a depth of 3—10 fathoms. But it also descends to a greater depth, and sometimes even to the lower limit of the named zone. It is a pelagic plant which prefers open shore, but also occurs on sheltered places and even enters the inner part of the great bays. Here it assumes, however, forms in general habit much differing from the pelagic and typical one. Such a form is figured by Kjellman in his N. Ish.

Algfl. t. 12, fig. 3. But I have often met with specimens which were still more narrow, with an almost linear and thread-narrow frond. Exceptionally this form has been found on open coast, but only on loose or clayish bottom. Thus I have taken it at Mehavn. On the other hand specimens are to be found with branches even 12 mm. in breadth in its broadest part. The species grows generally together with *Ptilota*, most often *Pt. pectinata*, or attached to this one, and also on the root of *Alaria* or *Laminaria*, more seldom on *Delesseria sinuosa*. It bears sporocarps in June, July and August, and tetraspores in August, although rather scarce. The greatest number of specimens collected by me in the named months were sterile. In Tromsö amt I have taken richly sporocarpiferous individuals at the end of August.

Distribution: Common and pretty plentiful all along the unsheltered coast, rather scarce in the inner part of the deeper bays.

Gen. Euthora J. G. Ag.
Alg. Liebm. p. 11; Spec. Alg. 2, p. 383.

Euthora cristata (L.) J. G. Ag.
l. c. Fucus cristatus L. in Turn. Hist. Fuc. 1, p. 48.

f. *typica*.

Descr. Euthora cristata J. G. Ag. Epicr. p. 360.
Fig. Rhodymenia cristata Harv. Phyc. Brit. t. 307.
Exsicc. Euthora cristata Aresch. Alg. Scand. exsicc. No. 308.

f. *angustata* Lyngb.
Hydr. Dan. p. 13.
Descr. Sphærococcus cristatus β angustatus Lyngb. l. c.

Syn. Fucus gigartinus Guun. Fl. Norv. 2, p. 106.
 „ cristatus Sommerf. Suppl. p. 184.
 „ coccineus β pusillus Wg. Fl. Lapp. p. 500.
Rhodymenia cristata Aresch. Phyc. Scand. p. 299.

Besides the typical form of this species there occurs a

narrow one, the above quoted f. *angustata* L y n g b. This form is analogous, to the before mentioned narrow form of *Odonthalia dentata* and *Rhodophyllis dichotoma*. It is on just the same or corresponding localities as these, that *Euthora cristata* cheafly assumes the form *angustata*. Also of this form I have seen almost thread narrow specimens with nearly linear branches, much differing from the typical one. According to my experience they pass, however, so gradually into each other, that no limit can be drawn between them.

The species in question is usually sublitoral, growing on stones, shells of Balanidæ, or more frepuently attached to other algæ, as *Laminaria hyperborea*, *Ptilota* and *Lithothamnia*, on a depth of 2—15 fathoms. Sometimes it occurs within the litoral zone, in rock-pools at low-water mark. It prefers open shore and appears scattered. The length rarely exceeds 4 cm. At East-Finmarken it has been taken with sporocarps in July and August; at West-Finmarken in May to September; in Tromsö amt in July and August; at Nordland during all the summer, according to K l e e n, and I have myself found it with such organs in September, Octoher and January. Tetrasporiferous specimens have been collected at East-Finmarken in August; at West-Finmarken in September; and at Nordland all the summer according to K l e e n.

Distribution; Commonly spread along the whole coast, and almost entering the inner end of the great bays.

Gen. **Rhodymenia** (Grev.) J. G. Ag.
Alg. Liebm. p. 15; Grev. Alg. Brit. p. 84; char. mut.

R h o d y m e n i a p a l m a t a (L.) Grev.
l. c. p. 93; Fucus palmatus L. Spec. Pl. 2, p. 1162.

f. *typica*.

α *nuda* Kjellm.
N, Ish. Algfl. p. 188.

Descr. Rhodymenia palmata f. typica α nuda Kjellm. N. Ish. Algfl. l. c.
   Fucus palmatus Turn. Hist. Fuc. 2, p. 114.
Fig.   „   „   Turn. l. c. t. 115, fig. a.

   β. *marginifera* (Turn.) Harv.
   Phyc. Brit. t. 217; Fucus palmatus β marginifera Turn. sec. Grev. Alg. Brit. p. 94.
Descr. Rhodymenia palmata f. typica β marginifera Kjellm. N. Ish. Algfl. p. 188.
Fig.   „   „   marginifera Harv. l. c.

   f. *sarniensis* Mert. (Grev.)
   Alg. Brit. p. 93; Fucus sarniensis Mert. in Roth, Cat. Bot. 3, p. 103.

   α. *latiuscula* Kjellm.
   N. Ish. Algfl. p. 189.
Descr. Rhodymenia palmata sarniensis J. G. Ag. Spec. Alg. 2, p. 377.
Fig. Sphærococcus sarniensis Kütz. Tab. Phyc. 18, t. 88.

   β. *tenuissima* Turn.
   Hist. Fuc. 1, p. 96.
Descr. Fucus sarniensis β tenuissima Turn. l. c.
Exsicc. Rhodymenia palmata var. sobolifera Aresch. Alg. Scand. exsicc. No. 155.

   f. *sobolifera* (Fl. Dan.) Harv.
   Phyc. Brit. t. 217; Fucus soboliferus Fl. Dan. t. 1065.
Descr. Rhodymenia palmata γ sobolifera J. G. Ag. Spec. Alg. 2, p. 377.
Fig. Fucus soboliferus Fl. Dan. l. c.
   Sphærococcus soboliferus Kütz. Tab. Phyc. 18, t. 90.

   f. *prolifera* Kütz.
   Sphærococcus palmatus γ prolifer Kütz. Spec. Alg. p. 781.
Descr. Rsodymenia palmata Aresch. Phyc. Scand. p. 298.
   „   „   f. prolifera α purpurea et β pallida Kjellm. N. Ish. Algfl. p. 189.
Exsicc.   „   „   Aresch. Alg. Scand. exsicc. No. 9.

   f. *angustifolia* Kjellm.
   N. Ish. Algfl. p. 189.
Descr. Rhodymenia palmata f. angustifolia Kjellm. l. c.

   Syn. Fucus ovinus Gunn. Fl. Norv. 1, p. 96 et Act. Nidros. p. 85, t. 9.
      „   palmatus Gunn. Fl. Norv. 2, p. 69.

Syn. Fucus bullatus Fl. Dan. t. 770.
„   foliaceus Ström in Act. Nidros. p. 347, t. 1. fig. 4.
„   caprinus Fl. Dan. t. 1128.
„   delicatulus Fl. Dan. t. 1190.
Ulva caprina Gunn. Fl. Norv. 2, p. 127.
„   delicatula Gunn l. c. p. 134, t. 8, fig. 2.
„   palmata Lyngb. Hydr. Dan. p. 24.
„   sobolifera Lyngb. l. c. p. 27.
„   „   Sommerf. in Act. Nidros. p. 50.

I cannot agree with Kjellman as to the f. *prolifera* α *purpuera* and β *pallida* being distinct. According to my experience they run gradually into each other without any limit. The one, α *purpurea*, is said to be a more northern form, the other, β *pallida*, a southern one, and differing only in colour. At Nordland I have often met with them, and there I have observed that f. *prolifera*, when growing in shallow rock-pools between tides, and not too much covered by other algæ, assumes as a rule the form *pallida*. But on the other hand, when it grows on the bottom of deeper shady pools or under dense mats of *Fucaceæ* it almost ever assumes the form *purpurea*, and sometimes it becomes rather thick or even leathery. The plant growing more or less free the colour gets paler, with complete transitions to both sides.

The present species is litoral as well as sublitoral. The typical form is, as far as I know, only litoral, or sometimes descends a little below extreme low-water mark. The form *sarniensis* I have only found in the sublitoral zone, sometimes on a depth of 3—4 fathoms, sometimes it descends to the lower limit of the zone, on a depth of about 20 fathoms. The form *prolifera* is generally litoral, but I have also taken it on a depth of 3—4 fathoms. The form *sobolifera* has been found at Finmarken by Vahl, but I do not know whether at East- or West-Finmarken. Sommerfelt has found this form at Bodö, and I have taken it in Lofoten. The plant occurs most commonly on rocks or stones, now and then attached to other algæ, as *Corallina* and *Fucaceæ*. It is best developed on open shore, but it is also to be met with on sheltered places or even at the inner end of deep bays (f. *sarniensis*). The length does not exceed 70 cm. Specimens with young tetrasporangia have been collected in the middle of July.

Distribution: Common and plentiful all along the shore and entering the inner end of the greater bays. On several localities it appears in great masses so as to determine essentially the character of the vegetation. However, the number of individuals generally seems to be less than at West-Finmarken.

Fam. **Gigartinaceæ** (Kütz.) J. G. Ag.
Epicr. p. 173; Kütz. Phyc. gener. p. 389; char. mut.

Gen. **Cystoclonium** Kütz.
Phyc. gener. p. 404.

Cystoclonium purpurascens (Huds.) Kütz.

l. c. Fucus purpurascens Huds. Fl. Angl. p. 589.
Descr. Cystoclonium purpurascens J. G. Ag. Epicr. p. 239.
Fig. Hypnea purpurascens Harv. Phys. Brit. t. 116.
Cystoclonium purpurascens Kütz. Tab. Phyc. 18, t. 15.
Exsicc.   „   „   Aresch. Alg. Scand. exsicc. No. 76.
Syn. Fucus confervoides Gunn. Fl. Norv. 2, p. 92.
   „   „   Wg. Fl. Lapp p. 504.
   „   elongatus Gunn. l. c. p. 143.
Cystoclonium purpurascens Kjellm. Ish. Algfl. p. 202.

A rather variable alga here as well as more southerly. I cannot find any limit at all between the typical form and the form *dendroidea* described by Kjellman after specimens from West-Finmarken. The plant is, as far as I have seen, always litoral, occurring mostly in rock-pools or on steep rocks. More seldom it is fastened to other algæ, as *Corallina*. It prefers open shore, but it is also to be met with on sheltered places. It is rather reduced in size, the length varying between 6 and 16 cm., generally 8—12. Specimens collected in the later half of June, in July and in the beginning of August have been sterile.

Distribution: Pretty common especially along the unsheltered part of the coast.

Gen. Kallymenia J. G. Ag.
Alg. Med. p. 98; Epicr. p. 219.

Kallymenia septemtrionalis Kjellm.
N. Ish. Algfl. p. 204.
Descr. Kallymenia septemtrionalis Kjellm. l. c.
Fig. „ „ „ „ t. 14, fig. 4—6.
Syn. Kallymenia reniformis Kleen, Nordl. Alg. p. 18.

Of late the present species has been considered by K j e l l- m a n as specifically distinct from *K. reniformis*. I have only once met with it at East-Finmarken. The specimens, collected in the beginning of August, were small, only 3—8 mm. It grew within the lower part of the sublitoral zone, on a depth of about 18 fathoms, attached to *Lithothamnia*.

Distribution: Only found at Lebesby on **Laxefjord**, rare.

Gen. Phyllophora (Grev.) J. G. Ag.
Alg. Med. p. 93; Grev. Alg. Brit. p. 135; lim. mut.

Phyllophora Brodiæi (Turn.) J. G. Ag.
l. c. Facus Brodiæi Turn. Hist. Fuc. 2, p. 1.
Descr. Phyllophora Brodiæi J. G. Ag. Epicr. p. 216.
Fig. „ „ Harv. Phyc. Brit. t. 20, fig. 1.
Exsicc. „ „ Aresch. Alg. Scand. exsicc. No. 207.

Sublitoral, sometimes growing in the uppermost part of

the zone, on a depth of 1—·2 fathoms, sometimes in the lower part on a depth of about 16 fathoms. It occurs on open coast as well as in the interior of deep bays, in scattered individuals.

Distribution: Probably sparingly spread along the whole coast. I have found it at Berlevaag and at Kirkenäs in Sydvaranger.

Gen. Ahnfeltia (Fr.) J. G. Ag.
Alg. Liebm. p. 12; Fr. Fl. Scand. p. 309; spec. excl.

Ahnfeltia plicata (Huds.) Fr.
l. c. p. 310; Fucus plicatus Huds. Fl. Angl. p. 589.
Descr. Ahnfeltia plicata J. G. Ag. Epicr. p. 206.
Fig. Gymnogongrus plicatus Harv. Phyc. Brit. t. 288.
Exsicc. Ahnfeltia plicata Aresch. Alg. Scand. exsicc. No. 77.

Syn. Fucus albus Gunn. Fl. Norv. 2, p. 92.
„ plicatus Wg. Fl. Lapp. p. 504.

At the only place where I met with this species, it grew in a rock-pool within the lower part of the litoral region, on much exposed shore. The couple of specimens I found were vigorous and well developed.

Distribution: Only found at Kjöllefjord, very rare.

Gen. Gigartina (Lamour.) J. G. Ag.
Epicr. p. 190; Lamour. Ess. p. 134; char. mut.

Gigartina mamillosa (Good. et Woodw.) J. G. Ag.
Alg. Med. p. 104; Fucus mamillosus Good. et Woodw. Linn. Trans. 3, p. 174.
Descr. Gigartina mamillosa J. G. Ag. Epicr. p. 199.
Fig. „ „ Harv. Phyc. Brit. t. 199.
Exsicc. „ „ Aresch. Alg. Scand. exsicc. No. 10.

Syn. Fucus spermophorus Gunn. Fl. Norv. 2, p. 26.
„ mamillosus Wg. Fl. Lapp. p. 469.
„ „ Sommerf. Suppl. p. 183.

Syn. Sphærococcus mamillosus Sommerf. in Act. Nidros p. 51.
Rhodymenia mamillosa Aresch. Phyc. Scand. p. 296.

Litoral, growing in rock-pools or most frequently on stones and rocks in the lower part of the zone. It is a pelagian plant which mainly occurs on open shore and best developed on much exposed places. Sometimes, however, it also penetrates into the deeper bays. Thus I found it at Kirkenæs in Sydvaranger pretty plentiful, but the specimens were small and somewhat stunted. It often grows gregarious in large number, for inst at Kjöllefjord and Finkongkjeilen, so as to determine considerably the character of the vegetation. I do not know when the species develops its reproductive organs, probably in the autumn. At West-Finmarken I have seen it bearing sporocarps in the later half of August and in September.

Distribution: In the western part of the district pretty common and abundant, in the eastern part less common and somewhat local, but at some places abundant, and enters pretty far into the deep fjords.

Gen. **Chondrus** (Stackh.) J. G. Ag.
Spec. Alg. 2, p. 244; Stackh. Ner. Brit. sec. J. G. Alg. . c.; char. mut.

Chondrus crispus (L.) Lyngb.
Hydr. Dan. p. 15; Fucus crispus L. Mant. p. 134.
Descr. Chondrus crispus J. G. Ag. Epicr. p. 178.
Fig.   „   „   Harv. Phyc. Brit. t. 63.
Exsicc. „   „   Aresch. Alg. Scand. exsicc. Nr. 156.
  Syn. Fucus crispus Gunn. Fl. Norv. 2, p. 91.
     „   „   Wg. Fl. Lapp. p. 497.
     „   norvegicus Gunn. l. c. p. 122. Cfr. Fosl. Krit. fort. p. 100.
  Eshara papyracea Strøm in Act. Nidros. p. 354.
  Chondrus crispus Lyngb. Hydr. Dan p. 15.
     „   norvegicus Lyngb. l. c. p. 16.

This alga I only have met with in the litoral region, partly in rock-pools, partly on stones and rocks in the lower part of the region, often at extreme low-water mark, on open coast as well as on sheltered places. It probably also descends into the sublitoral zone. Specimens found in June and July have been sterile, but in the middle of August bearing young tetrasporangia. At West-Finmarken I have collected it with tetrasporangia in the later half of July and in August; in Tromsö amt in May, and at Nordland in June, September and February.

Distribution: Scattered along the whole coast; at some places pretty common, as Kjöllefjord and Pasvig.

Fam. **Dumontiaceæ** J. G. Ag.
Epicr. p. 249.

Gen. **Halosaccion** (Kütz.) Rupr.
Alg. Och. p. 292; Kütz. Phyc. gener. p. 439; char. mut.

H a l o s a c c i o n r a m e͏́n t a c e u m (L.) J. G. Ag.
Spec. Alg. 2, p. 358; Fucus ramentaceus L. Syst. Nat. 2, p. 718.

f. *robusta* Kjellm.
N. Ish. Algfl. p. 196.

Descr. Halosaccion ramentaceum f. robusta Kjellm. l. c.
Fig.   „   „   „   „   l. c. t. 12, fig. 4 et
                                                  tab. 13. fig. 1—2.

f. *ramosa* Kjellm.
N. Ish. Algfl. p. 196.

Descr. Halosaccion ramentaceum f. ramosa Kjellm. l. c.
Fig.   „   „   „   „   „ t. 13, fig. 4.

α *major* Kjellm.
l. c.

β *minor* Kjellm.
l. c.

f. *subsimplex* Rupr.
Alg. Och. p. 270.
Descr. Halosaccion soboliferum var. subsimplex Rupr. l. c.
Fig. „ ramentaceum f. subsimplex Kjellm. Ish. Algfl. t. 13, fig. 3.

f. *densa* Kjellm.
N. Ish. Algfl. p. 196.
Descr. Scytosiphon ramentaceus Lyngb. Hydr. Dan. p. 61.
Fig. Fucus ramentaceus Turn. Hist. Fuc. t. 149.
Exsicc. Halosaccion ramentaceum Aresch. Alg. Scand. exsicc. No. 205.

    Syn. Fucus ramentaceus Gunn. Fl. Norv. 2, p. 79.
       „   „ Wg. Fl. Lapp. p. 504.
       „ barbatus Gunn. l. c. p. 129.
    Ulva sobolifera Gunn. l. c. p. 105.
    Scytosiphon ramentaceus Lyngb. Hydr. Dan. p. 61.
    Dumontia ramentacea Aresch. Phyc. Scand. p. 313.

This species is probably the most common of the Florideæ of East-Finmarken. It is also here somewhat variable, though it appears as a rule under the form *densa* along the open shore. This form grows gregarious in great number of individuals. Now and then f. *ramosa* and f. *subsimplex* are met with. The latter becomes mostly coarse on unsheltered coast, in quiet bays on the other hand, it gets much thinner. Of the form *robusta* I have not seen typical specimens at East-Finmarken, and here it seems to be very rare. A couple of specimens referred to this form are perhaps more really to be regarded as a transition between f. *densa* and f. *robusta*. Yet in Tromsö amt I have collected specimens which almost fully coincide with Spitzbergian ones, and therefore it is most likely to suppose, that it also occurs at Finmarken.

The present plant is litoral as well as sublitoral, yet it chiefly appears in the litoral zone. At some places it forms a broad girdle from about half tide to a few feet below extreme low-water mark. Sometimes it is attached to other algae, as *Fucaceae* in the litoral zone and roots of *Laminaria* in the sublitoral one. But it occurs particularly and best developed on rock-slopes at exposed places. Often it also is to be met with in rock-pools between tides. I do not know how far down it descends into the sublitoral region. The species probably develops its reproductive organs both in summer and in winter. In summer it is often found with the prolifications fallen off. Specimens with tetraspores have been collected in June, July and August; at West-Finmarken in May, June, July and August; and in Tromsö amt in July and October.

Distribution: Common and plentiful almost everywhere especially along the open coast.

Halosaccion pubescens nob.

H. thallo eramoso, subterete, apicem versus obsolote at basim versus valde et longe attenuato, subcartilagineo, prolificationibus simplicibus vel irregulariter romosis brevissimis undique deuse obsesso. Tab. 1 et tab. 2, fig. 1.

Syn. Halosaccion ramentaceum Fosl. herb.; ex parte.[1])

The species sometimes grows isolated, or more commonly several individuals rise from the same callus. The simple frond is after its whole length, except the lowest part, very densely covered with short simple or irregularly branched prolifications, and getting gradually shorter towards the top. These produce the tetrasporangia. Cp. pl. 1, the three figures to the right. The figure to the left shows a specimen, the prolifications of which for the greatest part are fallen off. By a cross section of the lower part of the frond, the cells of the outer layer are ordered in more or less regular series, being vertically rectangular with acute or rounded corners, more seldom squarish or roundish. The outermost cells are most often larger than the inner ones. In this manner it differs from other arctic species of the genus. Cp. S t r ö m f. Isl. Algfl. p. 30.

---

[1]) By this synonyme I only want to denote, that I have distributed some specimens of the present species under this name.

The present plant is litoral, growing in rock-pools on rather exposed shore Specimens collected in the later half of July were sparingly tetrasporiferous.

Distribution: Only found at Syltefjord, local, scarce.

Gen. **Dumontia** (Lamour.) J. G. Ag.
Spec. Alg. 2. p. 348, Lamour. Ess. p; 133; char. mut.

D u m o n t i a   f i l i f o r m i s (Fl. Dan.) Grev.
Alg. Brit. p. 165; Ulva filiformis Fl. Dan. t. 1480.

f. *typica*.
Descr. Dumontia filiformis J. G. Ag. Spec. Alg. 2, p. 349.
Fig. „ „ Harv. Phyc. Brit. t. 59 et 357 B.

f. *crispata* Grev.
Alg. Brit. p. 165.
Descr. Dumontia filiformis β crispata J. G. Ag. Spec. Alg. 2, p. 350.
Syn. Ulva filiformis Wg. Fl. Lapp. p. 508.
„ „ Sommerf. Suppl. p. 187.
Gastridium filiforme Sommerf. in Act. Nidros. p. 51.

The form *crispata*, as it appears at East-Finmarken, is not distinctly marked. Here it is narrower and less twisted than more southward, but on the other hand, it differs from f. *typica* by its greater firmness and by the inner layer of cells being larger. However, transitions are pretty common. It seems to prefer freshwater-streams between tides.

The present species is litoral, occurring most commonly in rock-pools or other caves between tides, attached to stones, shells or sometimes to *Fucaceae*. It often grows gregarious in rather considerable numbers, on open shore as well as in sheltered places, and it even enters the inner end of the greater bays. On much exposed places it becomes rather reduced in size. The largest specimens I have seen had a length of 35 cm., yet mostly smaller, sometimes only 5 cm. It has been taken with tetrasporangia in the later half of June, in July, and in the beginning of August (richly). I found a single specimen with sporocarps at the end of July.

Distribution: Commonly spread along the whole coast, at some places rather abundant. The form *crispata* collected at Mehavn, Nyborg and Bugönæs.

Fam. **Furcellariaceæ** J. G. Ag.
Epicr. p. 240.

Gen. **Furcellaria** Lamour.
Ess. p. 45.

Furcellaria fastigiata (L.) Lamour.
l. c. p. 46; Fucus fastigiatus L. Spec. Pl. 2, p. 1162.
Descr. Furcellaria fastigiata J. G. Ag. Epicr. p. 241.
Fig. „ „ Harv. Phyc. Brit t. 94 et 357 A.
Exsicc. „ „ Aresch. Alg. Scand. exsicc. No. 256.
Syn. Fucus fastigiatus Gunn. Fl. Norv. 1, p. 48.
„ furcellatus Gunn. l. c. 2, p. 78.
„ lumbricalis β Wg. Fl. Lapp. p. 503.

In my notes I have quoted a form of this species being found washed ashore at Mehavn. However I have not been able to find the specimens again in my collections brought home from East-Finmarken. Perhaps it was the form *tenuior* Aresch. Alg. Scand. exsicc. No. 257.

Distribution: Only found at Mehavn, very rare.

Fam. **Ceramiaceæ** (Ag.) Hauck.
Meeresalg. p. 16; Ag. Syst. Alg. p. XXVIII; char mut.

Gen. **Ceramium** (Lyngb.) Harv.
Man. p. 98; Lyngb. Hydr. Dan. p. 117; ex parte.

Ceramium strictum Grev. et Harv.
sec. Harv. Phyc. Brit. Syn. p. XI.

Descr. Ceramium strictum J. G. Ag. Epicr. p. 97.
Fig. „ „ Harv. Phyc. Brit. t. 334.
Exsicc. „ „ Hauck et Richt. Phyk. univ. No. 104.

The adding of this species to the Flora of East-Finmarken is founded only on a couple of badly preserved, sterile specimens from Sydvaranger. Typical specimens bearing tetrasporangia in the beginning of August have been taken at Russemark (Porsangerfjord) in West-Finmarken. Besides this I there also have collected a coarse and peculiar form of the present species.

Distribution: Unknown to me. A few specimens which are supposed to belong to the species in question have been found at Bugönæs in Sydvaranger.

Ceramium rubrum (Huds.) Ag.
Disp. Alg. p. 16; Conferva rubra Huds. Fl. Angl. p. 600.

f. *decurrens* J. G. Ag.
Spec. Alg. 2, p. 127.
Descr. Ceramium rubrum α decurrens J. G. Ag. Epicr. p. 100.
Exsicc. „ decurrens Aresch. Alg. Scand. exsicc. No. 208.

f. *genuina*.
Descr. Ceramium rubrum f. genuina Kjellm. N. Ish. Algfl. p. 214.

f. *prolifera* J. G. Ag.
Spec. Alg. 2, p. 127.
Descr. Ceramium rubrum β proliferum J. G. Ag. Epicr. p. 100.
Fig. „ secundatum Lyngb. Hydr. Dan. t. 37 A.
„ botryocarpum Harv. Phyc. Brit. t. 215.

f. *pedicellata* Duby.
sec. J. G. Ag. Spec. Alg. 2, p. 128.
Descr. Ceramium rubrum ε pedicellatum J. G. Ag. Epicr. p. 101.
Fig. „ „ Kütz. Tab. Phyc. 13; t. 4, fig. a—b.
Syn. Conferva littoralis Gunn. Fl. Norv. 2, p. 106.
„ rupestris Gunn. l. c. p. 107.
„ seposita Gunn. l. c. p. 116.
„ diaphana Wg. Fl. Lapp. p. 511.

This species appears at East-Finmarken almost ever under the forms *decurrens* and *genuina*, or forms which are most likely to be reckoned to either of them. Sometimes they are almost destitute of lateral branches, sometimes these branches are rather numerous, and then the forms approache more or less other forms of the species. Now and then I have met with specimens of f. *decurrens* reminding of *C. circinatum*, a plant rather common at some places in Nordland. I have only seen a few individuals of f. *prolifera* and f. *pedicellata*, the former at Kjelmö in Sydvaranger in rock-pools between tides, and the latter at Vadsö fastened to *Rhodomela lycopodioides* and the root of *Laminaria saccharina* within the sublitoral zone, on a depth of 5—8 fathoms.

The species in question occurs chiefly in rock-pools within the litoral zone, attached to stones or more commonly to *Corallina* and the smaller *Fucaceæ*, partly also to *Chondrus crispus*, *Halosaccion ramentaceum* and *Rhodomela lycopodioides*. It also descends into the sublitoral region, but here I have seldom met with it. Specimens with tetrasporangia have been found in July and August, with sporocarps in the later half of July and in August.

Distribution: Commonly spread along the whole coast, at some places, for inst Mehavn, plentiful.

Gen. **Ptilota** (Ag.) J. G. Ag.
Spec. Alg. 2, p. 92; Ag. Syn. Alg. p. XIX; ex parte.

Ptilota elegans Bonnem.
Hydr. loc. p. 22, sec. J. G. Ag. Spec. Alg. 2, p. 94.
Descr. Ptilota elegans J. G. Ag. Epicr. p. 74.
Fig. „ sericea Harv. Phyc. Brit. t. 191.
Exsicc. „ elegans Aresch. Alg. Scand. exsicc. No. 11.
„ plumosa Wyatt, Alg. Danm. No. 77.

Litoral and sublitoral. Within the latter zone it probably has a scanty distribution. I only once found it there, attached to stones on a depth of about 5 fathoms. Within the litoral zone it generally occurs on steep rocks covered by other algæ, as *Fucus* and *Ozothallia*, or on the walls of grotto-shaped cavities most often together with *Delesseria alata*. It is only to be found on open shore and best developed in much exposed localities. Even as far eastward as at Vardö I have seen very luxuriant individuals about 15 cm. high. However it is most commonly smaller, 4—8 cm. Specimens bearing only few tetrasporangia have been collected in the later half of July and in the earlier half of August.

Distribution: Pretty common along the unsheltered part of the coast, at some places abundant but local.

Ptilota plumosa (L.) Ag.

Syn. Alg. p. 39. excl β; Fucus plumosus L. Mant. p. 134.
Descr. Ptilota plumsa J. G. Ag. Epicr. p. 75.
Fig. „ „ Harv. Phyc. Brit. t. 80.
Exsicc. „ Aresch. Alg. Scand. exsicc. No. 160.
  Syn. Fucus plumosus Gunn. Fl. Norv. 2, p. 91.
     „ ptilotus Gunn. l. c. p. 135.
     „ cartilagineus Gunn. l. c. p. 108; ex parte.
     „ „ vindicatus Gunn. l. c. p. 123; ex parte.
     „ plumosus α et β Wg. Fl. Lapp. p. 501

A generally sublitoral alga, occurring on a depth of 2—16 fathoms. Sometimes it appears in rock pools within the litoral zone attached to roots of *Laminaria*. Best developed and most abundant it is to be met with on stony or rocky bottom on open coast, on a depth of 5—10 fathoms, attached partly to the rock itself, partly to the stem of *Alaria* and *Laminaria*, especially *L hyperborea*. Particularly at Berlevaag and Vardö I have collected very luxuriant specimens, which had a length of 30—35 cm. On some localities it grows gregarious in rather large number. It appears also in the greater bays or else in sheltered localities, but here it never becomes so vigorously developed as on the unsheltered coast. The plant bears tetrasporangia in June, July and August; sporocarps at the end of May, in June, July and August.

Distribution: Common along the whole coast, at several places abundant but somewhat local.

Ptilota pectinata (Gunn.) Kjellm.

N. Ish. Algfl. p. 219; Fucus pectinatus Gunn. Fl. Norv. 2, p. 122.

f. *typica*.

α *distans* nob.

Descr. Ptilota serrata J. G. Ag. Epicr. p. 76.
Fig. „ plumosa var. serrata Kütz. Tab. Phyc. 12, t. 55.
Exsicc. „ serrata Aresch. Alg Scand. exsicc. No. 406.

β *densa* nob.

f. laxe cæspitosa, 4—8 cm. alta; ramis confertis, parce serratis vel integris.

f. *Kjellmani* nob.

Descr. Ptilota pectinata f. litoralis Kjellm. N. Ish. Algfl. p. 219.
Fig. „ „ „ „ l. c. t. 15, fig. 2—5.
Syn. Fucus plumosus γ tenerrimus Wg. Fl. Lapp. p. 501.
Ptilota plumosa β asplenoides Lyngb. Hydr. Dan. p. 38.

It has been shown by Kjellman that *Pt. serrata* Kütz. is identic with the plant formerly described and figured by Gunnerus under the name of *Fucus pectinatus*. And I have lately stated the occurrens of the species in Gunnerus' herbarium under this name, with exception of a single specimen, which belongs to *Pt. plumosa*.[1]

The form described and named by Kjellman f. *litoralis* also occurs in East-Finmarken. Besides this there is to be found within the litoral region another form, which

---

[1] There is a considerable misprint in my Krit. fort. p. 103 in reference to the specimens of *Pt. pectinata* in the herbarium of Gunnerus. Instead of „hvoraf et tilhörer den form af *Pt. plumosa*, der har karakter af begge arter", there must be read „hvoraf et tilhörer *Pt. plumosa*" („one of which belongs to *Pt. plumosa*").

is an intermediate one between f. *litoralis* and f. *typica*, yet most likely to be reckoned to the latter. I therefore propose to call the former f. *Kjellmani*, and the latter I have called f. *typica* β *densa*. The form *Kjellmani*, as already mentioned by Kjellman, by a cursory examination reminds of *Pt. elegans*, and sometimes grows jointly with this species. It reaches a length of 8 cm. Rather similar to f. *Kjellmani* in general habit and equal in size is f. *typica* β *densa*, which, as above mentioned, also appears within the litoral zone, but never jointly with, or as far as I have seen, on such localities as this one. It differs from f. *typica* α *distans* by being somewhat tufted, though not always, and by its smallness and far denser branching. Sometimes it becomes almost as slender as f. *Kjellmani*. As for the structure too it is most likely related to f. *typica* α *distans*, although I have not, in this respect, seen any real limit between the forms of the present species. Cp. Kjellm. N. Ish. Algfl. p. 221, t. 15, fig. 4—6. The form is generally litoral, pelagian and occurs mostly in rock-pools within the lower part of the zone. But it is also to be found in the upper part of the sublitoral zone, on a depth of 2—4 fathoms, and here I have met with every transition between this form and the form *distans*. I have also seen this form from Marblehead, Mass., N. America.

The form α *distans* is sublitoral as well as elitoral. It grows in scattered individuals and chiefly on hard stony or shingly bottom on open coast. But it has also been collected on looser bottom and in sheltered localities, though it here never seems to thrive. Most vigorously developed it appears on a depth of 8—15 fathoms on unsheltered coast. In the elitoral zone I have found isolated specimens on a depth of about 25 fathoms.

The plant becomes never so large and luxuriant as the preceding one. The largest specimens I have seen had a length of about 25 cm., but it is commonly much smaller.

It has been found with tetrasporangia in June, July and August, in the later month however sparingly; with sporacarps at the end of May, in June, July and August.

Distribution: Commonly spread along the whole coast; at some places rather common but not plentiful.

Gen. **Callithamnion** (Lyngb.) Thur.
in Le Jol. Liste Alg. Cherb. p. 17; Lyngb. Hydr. Dan. p. 123; lim. mut.

C a l l i t h a m n i o n s c o p u l o r u m Ag.
Spec. Alg. 2, p. 166.
Descr. Callithamnion scopulorum J. G. Ag. Spec. Alg. 2. p. 47.
Fig. „   „   Kütz. Tab. Phyc. 11, t. 70.
  „ roseum β tenue Lyngb. Hydr. Dan. t. 39.

Litoral, occurring on steep rocks on open shore, and often jointly with *Sphacelaria olivacea*, *Ptilota elegans* and *Delesseria alata*. When growing isolated, it forms small roundish and sometimes confluent tufts. With respect to the ramification it is very nearly related to the form of *C. polyspermum* found at Nordland and West-Finmarken. Cp. Kjellm. Ish. Algfl. p. 223. But the present species has another general habit than that one, and it never grows epiphytic on other algæ. J. G. A g a r d h has had the kindness to examine it, and he finds it agreeing pretty well with the original specimen of L y n g b y e in the herbarium of C. A. A g a r d h. The only difference is, that L y n g b y e's specimen is a litte shorter, with shorter cells, and more robust, and therefore more densely branched. It reaches a length of 3 cm., most commonly about 2 cm. Specimens collected in the earlier half of August were tetrasporiferous. At West-Finmarken I have taken it with tetrasporangia in the earlier half of September.

Distribution: Only found at Vardö, pretty plentiful but local.

Gen. **Antithamnion** (Näg.) Thur.

in Le Jol. Liste Alg. Cherb. p. 111; Näg. Algensyst. p. 200; char. mut.

Antithamnion floccosum (Müll.) Kleen.

Nordl. Alg. p. 11; Conferva floccosa Müll. Fl. Dan. t. 328. fig. 1.

f. *atlantica* J. G. Ag.

Descr. Callithamnion floccosum var. α atlanticum J. G. Ag. Epicr. p. 22.
Fig. „ „ Harv. Phyc. Brit. t. 81.

This alga is litoral as well as sublitoral. In the litoral zone it occurs on rocks at low-water, covered by other algæ, or in deep and shady rock-pools between tides, most rarely epiphytic. I have found a solitary specimen on *Rhodomela lycopodioides* and on *Halosaccion ramentaceum*, in the latter case in a rock-pool where both species grew side by side in rather considerable abundance. Scattered individuals have also been found attached to *Lithothamnia* within the sublitoral region on a depth of 3—5 fathoms. It seems not to descend to a greater depth. The plant appears almost only on open shore, and it thrive best in much exposed localities, growing spread, or sometimes gregarious in considerable number. The specimens are generally small. But at Syltefjord I met with luxuriant ones reaching a length of 8 cm., and at Berlevaag I found it in great number on an iron buoy, which was laid out in the summer 1885, and put on shore for cleaning in July 1887. The greatest part of the specimens here collected were large and well developed, attaining 10 cm. in length. Here the plant grew associated with *Antithamnion boreale*, *A. Pylaisæi*, *Polysiphonia urceolata* and a few other algæ.

The present plant has usually been found sterile. But those specimens collected at Berlevaag, in the middle of July, were richly tetrasporiferous, yet only a few of them fully developed. It has been found at Scotland bearing sporocarps in April and May. Cp. Traill, Monogr. Appendix.

Distribution: Generally scattered and scanty along the

whole coast; at some places, as Berlevaag and Syltefjord, abundant but local.

Antithamnion Pylaisæi (Mont.) Farl.

New. Engl. Alg. p. 123; Callithamnion Pylaisæi Mont. Pl. Cell. No. 11, sec. J. G. Ag. Epicr. p. 22.

f. *typica*,

Descr. Callithamnion Pylaisæi Harv. Ner. Bor. Am. 2, p. 239.
         • (Antithamnion) Pylaisæi Farl. New. Engl. Alg. p. 123.
Fig. Callithamnion Pylaisæi Harv. Ner. Bor. Am. 2, t. 36 B.
         •   „ Kütz. Tab. Phyc. 11, t. 90.

f. *norvegica* Kjellm.

N. Ish. Algfl. p. 225.
Descr. Antithamnion Pylaisæi f. norvegica Kjellm. l. c.
Fig.   „   „   „   „   „ t. 16, fig. 1.

The most common form of this species grows generally scattered, often with isolated, small individuals, 0.5—1 cm. in height, as to the shape and position of the branches most nearly agreeing with fig. 3—4 on pl. 36 B in Harv. Ner. Bor. Am. However the cells of the main axis and of the long branches are shorter than in American specimens according to Harvey. The length does not exceed 4 times the diameter, generally 2—3. I have seldom seen specimens with as patent and rather blunt branches as the form figured by Kjellman l. c. On the iron buoy at Berlevaag mentioned under *A. floccosum*, I met with rather luxuriant individuals reaching a height of 5 cm. They resemble Harvey's fig. 1 l. c., or sometimes more densely branched, and almost fully coincide with American specimens determined by Farlow, only smaller and a little darker. The cells of the main axis and partly of the long branches are up to 6 times longer than the diameter. These specimens I have referred to the typical form, and most af the above mentioned smaller ones with short cells and somewhat patent branches I have referred to f. *norvegica*. The latter I think to be only a stunted one produced by unfavourable conditions of life, and it passes gradually into the typical form without any limit.

The present plant is at East-Finmarken, as far as I have seen, always sublitoral, and appears in the upper as well as in the lower part of the zone, attached to *Lithothamnia* and shells of Balanidæ. Solitary specimens have also been found fastened to *Delesseria sinuosa*, *Ptilota plumosa* and the root-tuft of *Polysiphonia arctica*. Sometimes it grows gregarious but not in large number. It is best developed in much exposed localities, and does not enter into the deeper bays. I have collected specimens with tetrasporangia in the middle of June at Kjöllefjord, rather richly; at Mehavn at the end of June, sparingly; and at Berlevaag in the middle of July, rather richly.

Distribution: Commonly spread but scarce along the unsheltered coast; at Berlevaag found in considerable abundance on an iron buoy.

Antithamnion boreale Gobi (Kjellm.)
N. Ish. Algfl. p. 226; Antithamnion plumula var. boreale Gobi, Algenfl. Weiss. Meer. p. 47.

f. *typica* Kjellm.
N. Ish. Algfl. p. 226.
Descr. Antithamnion plumula var. boreale Gobi l. c. p. 47 et sequent.
Fig. „ boreale f. typica Kjellm. l. c. t. 16, fig. 2—3.

f. *corallina* Rupr. (Kjellm.)
Descr. Callithamnion corallina Rupr. Alg. Och. p. 340.
Antithamnion corallina Kjellm. Algenw. Murm. Meer. p. 24.
Fig. „ boreale f. corallina Kjellm. N. Ish. Algfl. t. 16, fig. 4—5.
Syn. Antithamnion plumula Kjellm. Spetsb. Thall. 1, p. 26.

I have only seen a comparatively small number of this species, and especially at East-Finmarken it is dwarfed, seldom, if ever, reaching more than 3—4 cm. in height, most commonly about 1 cm. It is often very difficult to distinguish from *A. Pylaisæi*, particularly when growing together with that species, and this is not seldom the case. In my collections I have specimens which, as far as I am able to judge, may be referred to either of these two species.

The plant is sublitoral, occurring partly in the upper part of the region, on a depth of 2—5 fathoms, partly on a depth of about 15 fathoms. It prefers exposed localities and has not been met with in the deeper bays, usually growing scattered, attached to shells of Balanidæ, *Lithothamnia*, *Rhodophyllis dichotoma*, *Ptilota plumosa* and *pectinata*. Specimens bearing tetrasporangia, but sparingly, have been collected at Kjöllefjord in the middle of June; at Mehavn in the beginning of July, also sparingly (f. *corallina*); at Berlevaag in the middle of July, rather richly; and at Kjelmö in Sydvaranger in the beginning of August, very sparingly.

Some specimens collected at Kjelmö are densely overgrown with small cysts with oily contents, probably *Chytridium plumulæ* C o h n.

Distribution: Scattered and in general very scarce along the unsheltered coast; rather common on an iron buoy at Berlevaag (f. *typica*). A few specimens of f. *corallina* found at Mehavn, and at Kjelmö a transition between this form and f. *typica*.

Gen. **Rhodochorton** Näg.
Ceram. p. 121.

Subgen. 1. **Thamnidium** Thur.
in Le Jol. Liste Alg. Cherb. p. 110.

R h o d o c h o r t o n   R o t h i i (Turt.) Näg.
Ceram. p. 121; Conferva Rothii Turt. Syst. 6, p. 1806, sec. Dillw. Brit. Conf. t. 73.

f. *typica*.
Descr. Callithamnion Rothii J. G. Ag. Epicr. p. 13.
Fig. Thamnidium Rothii Thur. in Le Jol. Liste Alg. Cherb. t. 5.
Exsicc.   „   „   Aresch. Alg. Scand. exsicc. No. 259.

f. *globosa* Kjellm.

N. Ish. Algfl. p. 232.
Descr. Rhodochorton Rothii f. globosa Kjellm. l. c.
Fig. „ „ „ „ „ t. 15, fig. 9—13.
Syn. Callithamnion Rothii Lyngb. Hydr. Dan. p. 121, t. 41 A.
  „   floridulum Lyngb. l. c. p. 121, t. 41 D.
  „   „   Sommerf. Suppl. p. 193.
  „   Rothii Sommerf. Suppl. p. 193 et in Act. Nidros. p. 51.

Litoral and sublitoral. Within the litoral zone the typical form occurs on rocks, forming more or less dense mats often together with *Sphacelaria olivacea*. Within the sublitoral zone it is met with on a depth of 3—8 fathoms, attached to *Lithothamnia*, *Laminaria* and other algæ. It appears on open coast as well as in sheltered places, and sometimes gregarious in considerable abundance. The form *globosa* has been found on rocks within the litoral zone, and fastened to *Lithothamnia* within the sublitoral zone, on open coast. I have sometimes met with a form reminding of *Rh. intermedium* K j e l l m., with the cells 5—8 times the diameter, but sterile. Specimens with young tetrasporangia have been collected at the end of June, and at West-Finmarken ripe ones at the end of September.

Distribution: Commonly distributed along the whole coast; at some places, as Sværholt, Berlevaag and Vardö, abundant but local; f. *globosa* found at Sværholt and Vardö.

R h o d o c h o r t o n (?) s p a r s u m (Carm.) Kjellm.

N. Ish. Algfl. p. 234; Callithamnion sparsum Carm. in Hook. Brit. Fl. p. 348.
Descr. Callithamnion sparsum J. G. Ag. Epicr. p. 14.
Fig. „   „ Harv. Phyc. Brit. t. 297.
Syn. Thamnidium sparsum Kleen, Nordl. Alg. p. 23.

Sublitoral, found on decaying stems of *Laminaria hyperborea*.

Distribution: Only found at Sværholt and Syltefjord, rare.

Subgen. 2. **Thamniscus** Kjellm.
Spetsb. Thall. 1, p. 29.

Rhodochorton mesocarpum (Carm.) Kjellm.
N. Ish. Algfl. p. 234; Callithamnion mesocarpum Carm. in Hook. Brit. Fl. 2, p. 348.

f. *penicilliformis* Kjellm.
Spetsb. Thall. 1, p. 30.
Descr. Thamnidium mesocarpum f. penicilliformis Kjellm. l. c.
    Rhodochorton   „   „   „ N. Ish. Algfl. p. 235.
Fig.   „   „   „   „ l. c. t. 16, fig. 6—7.

Litoral and sublitoral, epiphytic on other algæ, as *Chætomorpha melagonium*, *Halosaccion ramentaceum*, *Ptilota plumosa* and *pectinata*. It seems to be best developed on exposed places, but has also been found in sheltered localities, though never in the deeper bays. Specimens with tetrasporangia have been collected in the middle of June and at the end of August.

Distribution: Scattered along the unsheltered part of the coast but very scarce (Sværholt, Kjöllefjord, Mehavn, Havningberg).

Fam. **Wrangeliaceæ** (J. G. Ag.) Hauck.
Meeresalg. p. 14; J. G. Ag. Spec. Alg. 2, p. 701; lim. mut.

Gen. **Chantransia** (D. C.) Fries.
Syst. Veg. p. 338; DC. Fl. Fr. 2, p. 49, lim. mut.

Chantransia efflorescens (J. G. Ag.) Kjellm.
Spetsb. Thall. 1, p. 4; Callithamnion efflorescens J. G. Ag. Spec. Alg. 2, p. 15.

f. *tenuis* Kjellm.

N. Ish. Algfl. p. 166.
Descr. Chantransia efflorescens f. tenuis Kjellm. l. c.
Fig. „ „ „ „ l. c. t. 12, fig. 1—2.

I have met with this species only once. It grew fastened to *Chætomorpha melagonium* within the upper part of the sublitoral zone, on a depth of about 3—5 fathoms.

Distribution: Only found at Sværholt, rare. I think it more commonly spread along the open part of the coast.

Chantransia Daviesii (Dillw.) Thur.
in Le Jol. Alg. mar. Cherb. p. 106; Conferva Daviesii Dillw. Brit·
Conf. Intr. p. 73.
Descr. Callithamnion Daviesii J. G. Ag. Epicr. p. 8.
Fig. „ „ Harv. Phyc. Brit. t. 314.
Exsicc. Chantransia „ Hauck et Richter, Phyk. univ. No. 59.

I found a few sparingly branched and barren specimens of a *Chantransia*, appearing to belong to this species. They grew epiphytic on *Sphacelaria arctica* within the litoral zone.

Distribution: Only found at Sværholt and Syltefjord, rare.

Chantransia virgatula (Harv.) Thur.
in Le Jol. Alg. mar. Cherb. p. 106; Callithamnion virgatulum Harv.
in Hook. Brit. Fl. 2, p. 349.
Descr. Chantransia virgatula Hauck, Meeresalg. p. 39.
Fig. „ „ Harv. Phyc. Brit. t. 313.
  Trentepohlia „ Farl. New. Engl. Alg. t. 10, fig. 3.
  Callithamnion virgatulum Kütz. Tab. Phyc. 11, t. 56.
Exsicc. „ „ Wyatt, Alg. Danm. Nr. 189.
Syn. Chantransia virgatula f. Farlowii Kjelm. N. Ish. Algfl. p. 167

As citied by Kjellman (l. c.) one of the forms of this species, found in the Norwegian Polar Sea, seems no doubt identic with the form described and figured by Farlow under the name of *Trentepohlia virgatula*, and this form again I consider to be identic with Kützing's *Callithamnion piliferum* from Bretagne (Tab. Phyc. l. c.). Farlow quotes his species as being identical with Harvey's *Callithamnion virgatulum* Phyc. Brit. t. 313. Kjellman, however, records it as a distinct form, f. *Farlowii*, and he says: «The two figures (Farlow's and Harvey's) are very different from each other, so as to make the impression that the two authors by one and the same name have meant specifically distinct algæ».

Having seen a considerable number of this species at East-Finmarken as well as at West-Finmarken I must agree with Farlow considering his *T. virgatula* to be so nearly related to *C. virgatulum* Harv. that, as far as I can judge, it cannot even be maintained as a distinct form. The essential difference between the two figures is, according to my apprehension, that Harvey's plant is wanting the rather numerous and long hairs, but, on the contrary, bears numerous short branches, consisting as it seems of a single cell. These are, on the other hand, proportionally few on the specimen figured by Farlow, and still fewer on Kützing's figure. At Finmarken I have met with specimens bearing numerous secondary branches consisting of 1—3 cells, though not as numerous as on fig. 3 by Harvey. By other ones these branches are almost wanting, the plant being sporiferous or not. And thus too with regard to the hairs. By some specimens these appear rather abundant, by others quite wanting, in which case the plant almost fully is corresponding with fig. 3—4 by Harvey.[1] The figures in Phyc. Brit. are drawn from a richly sporiferous specimen, and, therefore, I suppose it to be likely that some of the apparently secondary branches on fig. 2 have been spores or such organs in development.

Harvey states that the species sometimes is difficult to be distinguished from *Ch. Daviesii*. It is, in fact, rather variable, but I never saw any transition between these two.

[1]. With reference to the division of the spores cp. Näg. Ceram. p. 170.

However, the forms, as far as I have seen, are running so gradually into each other that no limit can be drawn between them. In Manual (Ed. 2, p. 184) H a r v e y unites the present species with *Ch. Daviesii*, but in Phyc. Brit. it is again kept distinct, and he refers to W y a t t, Alg. Danm. No. 189. The plant here distributed I find most essentially coinciding with the form or forms in the Norwegian Polar Sea.

The species in question is 2—4 mm. high, and the cells have a thickness of 12—14 µ. It has been found with reproductive organs at East-Finmarken in July and August, and at West-Finmarken in September. The spores are almost ever solitary, partly sessile and scattered along the branches without any distinct order, partly on a short shaft consisting of 1—3 cells, or sometimes in the angle between a short secondary branch and its main axis. The plant is litoral as well as sublitoral. Within the latter zone it has only been found on a depth of 2—3 fathoms. It appears best developed on exposed places but occurs also in sheltered localities, attached to *Cystoclonium purpurascens*, *Rhodymenia palmata*, *Rhodomela lycopodioides*, *Alaria*, *Cladophora gracilis* and sometimes also *Antithamnion floccosum*.

Distribution: Found at Sværholt, rather scarce; at Mehavn, rare; and at Vardö, local but abundant.

C h a n t r a n s i a s e c u n d a t a (Lyngb.) Thur.

in Le Jol. Liste Alg. Cherb. p. 106; Callithamnion Daviesii β ecundatum Lyngb. Hydr. Dan. p. 129.
Descr. Chantransia secundata Hauck, Meeresalg. p. 41; excl. syn. plur.
Fig. Callithamnion secundatum Kütz. Tab. Phyc. 11, t. 56.
Exsicc. Trentepohlia secundata Aresch. Alg. Scand. exsicc. Nr. 84.

Litoral, growing on *Porphyra laciniata* and *Diploderma amplissimum*. It has been found with spores in the beginning of August.

Distribution: Only found at Vardö and Mehavn, rare.

Chantransia microscopica (Näg.) nob.
Callithamnion microscopicum Näg in Kütz. Spec. Alg. p. 640.
Descr. Achrochaetium microscopicum Näg. Ceram. p. 173.
Fig. „ „ Näg. l. c. fig. 24—25.
Callithamnion „ Kütz. Tab. Phyc. 11, t. 58.

This species appears to be considered as a distinct one. From *Ch. secundata* it distinguishes itself most essentially by its vertical threads arising from a disk consisting of one cell, which is, seen from above, shaped like a ring. By *Ch. secundata* the threads arise from a cellular base. I have found this to be constant by all the specimens I have seen, and Nägeli says (l. c. p. 173) that «ein mehrcelliger Discus wie bei den übrigen Arten ist nicht vorhanden».

The present plant is litoral, growing in rock-pools epiphytic on *Polysiphonia urceolata*, on rather exposed places. The Finmarkian specimens are smaller (50—100 µ long, the cells 6—8 µ thick) and less branched than those figured by Kützing. The hairs are also much fewer. It bears reproductive organs at the end of July.

Distribution: Only found at Kjelmö in Sydvaranger, rare.

Fam. **Hildbrandtiaceae** Hauck.
Meeresalg. p. 13.

Gen. Hildbrandtia Kütz.
Isis 1834, p. 675.

Hildbrandtia rosea Kütz.
Phyc. gener. p. 384.
Descr. Hildbrandtia rosea J. G. Ag. Epicr. p. 379.
Fig. „ „ Kütz. Tab Phyc. 19, t. 91.
Exsicc. „ „ Aresch. Alg. Scand. exsicc. Nr. 159.

Litoral, growing in rock-pools or on rocks, chiefly within the lower part of the zone. It seems to prefer open shore,

At East-Finmarken I have collected specimens with spores at the end of July, and it has been taken with such organs at West-Finmarken in the middle of August and in September.

Distribution: Scattered along the whole coast, at some places pretty common.

Fam. Squamariaceæ (Zanard.) Hauck

Meeresalg. p. 18; Zanard. Synops. p. 133, sec. J. G. Ag. Spec. Alg. 2, p. 285; lim. mut.

Gen. Actinococcus Kütz.
Phyc. Gen. p. 177.

Actinococcus roseus (Suhr) Kütz.
l. c.; Rivularia rosea Suhr, sec. Kütz. l. c.
Descr. Actinococcus roseus J. G. Ag Spec. Alg. 2, p. 489.
Fig. " " Kütz. Phyc. gen. t. 45, fig. IV.
" " " Tab. Phyc. 1, t. 31.

Sublitoral, growing epiphytic on *Phyllophora Brodiæi* on a depth of about 16 fathoms. I have only seen a couple of specimens from East-Finmarken, taken in August. At West-Finmarken it has been collected in June and in September.

Distribution: Only found at Kirkenæs in Sydvaranger, very rare.

Gen. Petrocelis J. G. Ag.
Spec. Alg. 2, p. 489.

Petrocelis Middendorffi (Rupr.) Kjellm.
N. Isb. Algfl. p. 180; Cruoria Middendorffi Rupr. Alg. Oct. p. 329.
Descr. Cruoria Middendorffi Rupr. l. c. sub. Cruoria pellita.
Petrocelis " Kjellm. l. c.
Fig. Cruoria pellita Rupr. l. c. t. 18, fig. a—b.

I have once met with a solitary barren specimen of a

Petrocelis, which I suppose belongs to this species. It grew on a stone in the sublitoral zone, on a depth of about 3 fathoms.

Distribution: A single specimen found at Mehavn.

Fam. **Porphyraceæ** (Kütz.) Thur.

in Le Jol. Liste Alg. Cherb. p. 16; Kütz. Phyc. gener. p. 382; char. mut.

Gen. **Diploderma** Kjellm.
N. Ish. Algfl. p. 236.

Diploderma amplissimum Kjellm.
N. Ish. Algfl. p. 236.

f. *planiuscula* nob.

    f. plana vel parce undulato-plicata; thalli parte media 40—60 μ crassa, cellulis in sectione tran-versa quadratis vel verticaliter subrectangularibus.
Exsicc. Porphyra miniata Aresch. Alg. Scand. exsicc. Nr. 262.

f. *typica*.
Descr. Diploderma amplissimum Kjellm. l. c.
Fig.   „   „   „   „ t. 17, fig. 1—3; t. 18, fig. 1—8.

f. *tenuissima* Strömf. (nob.)
Descr. Diploderma tenuissimum Strömf. Isl. Alveg. p. 33.
Fig.   „   „   „ l. c. t. 1, fig. 17—18.
Exsicc. Cfr. Porphyra miniata Collins in Hauck et Richt. Phyk. univ. No. 8.
    Syn. Ulva umbilicalis β purpurea Wg. Fl. Lapp. p. 506.
        Porphyra laciniata f. linearis et vulgaris Kleen, Nordl. Alg. p. 23.
        „   coccinea Kleen l. c. p. 24.
        „   miniata Aresch. Phyc. Scand. p. 407; ex parte.

This species, as understood in the above taken sense, includes several forms rather different, but on the other hand nearly connected. Thus *D. tenuissimum* S t r ö m f. in my opinion is but a form of *D. amplissimum*. At East-Finmarken I have collected specimens which fully coincide with Icelandic ones in habit as well as structure, being 25 μ thick with, in cross section, horizontally rectangular cells. But it passes gradually into *D. amplissimum* f. *typica*, which has squarish or vertically rectangular cells by a thickness usually varying between 50 and 60 µ., sometimes a little thicker, sometimes thinner. In H a u c k et R i c h t. Phyk. univ. Nr. 8 such an intermediate form is distributed by C o l l i n s under the name of *Porphyra miniata*. It has the outward appearance of *D. amplissimum* f. *typica* but it is, at the middle part of the frond, only 36 µ thick, and the cells are, in cross section, horizontally rectangular, resembling fig. 18 by S t r ö m f e l t l. c. Another specimen from Nahant, Mass., communicated to me by C o l l i n s, coincides almost fully with the typical form of *D. tenuissimum*. The frond is at the middle 25 µ. thick. I therefore think *D. tenuissimum* ought to be regarded as a form of *D. amplissimum*.

The typical form of *D. amplissimum* is distinguishing itself by its darker colour, greater thickness and especially by its being densely folded, «often so deeply that the folds extend to the middle line of the frond». However from this deep folding it passes gradually into quite smooth, and then it approaches much to *D. miniatum* (Lyngb.).[1] Such a form

---

[1]. I have only seen a single specimen of *D. miniatum*, which I found some years ago at Gjesvær in West-Finmarken, attached to the rudder of a smaller vessel then carrying trade between Gjesvær and Hammerfest. I suppose this vessel the preceding year has been in the neighbourhood of Spitzbergen, and there the spore has fastened itself to the rudder, because the species has not been found earlier nor later at the coast of Norway. I have not succeeded in getting accurate informations as to the route of the vessel that year.

The specimen in question accords well with the description given by L y n g b y e in Hydr. Dan. t. 29, and the figures by K ü t z i n g in Tab. Phyc. 19, t. 81, and K j e l l m a n in N. Isb. Algfl. t. 18, fig. 9. The margin is irregularly laciniate and somewhat denticulate, and the middle of the frond has a thickness of 72 µ. The specimen was collected in the beginning of September, bearing sporocarps and antheridia. Thus this plant is not always dioecious. Cp. K j e l l m. N, Ish, Algfl. p. 238.

I think *Porphyra miniata* A r e s c h. Alg. Scand. exsicc. Nr. 262 to be, the above quoted f. *planiuscula*, or at least most nearly related to *D. amplissimum*.[1] The frond is 62 µ thick, and the cells are, in cross section, squarish or sometimes rectangular, but never attaining the height in propostion to the length as those of f. *typica*. The colour is generally a little paler than by the typical form, or between f. *tenuissima* and f. *typica*. I have the same form from Stavanger and from Lödingen in Nordland. I also met with it at East-Finmarken, though not quite typical, but mostly transitions between this form and f. *typica*.

The present plant is as a rule sublitoral, occurring on a depth of 1—6 fathoms fastened to other algæ, but sometimes it also lives in the lowermost part of the litoral zone. Loosened specimens are often met with in the later half of July and in August, floating on the surface of the water, or washed ashore in considerable numbers. It prefers open coast but it is also met with in sheltered localities, and it sometimes penetrates even pretty far into the greater fjords, for inst. at Lebesby on Laxefjord. Individuals bearing sporocarps and antheridia have been collected at the end of June, in July and the earlier half of August.

Distribution: Common almost everywhere along the unsheltered part of the coast and at some places abundant, for inst. Mehavn and Vardö.

Gen. **Porphyra** Ag.
Syst. Alg. p. XXXII.

P o r p'h y r a l a c i n i a t a (Lightf.) Ag.
l. c. p. 190; Ulva laciniata Lightf. Fl. Scot. p. 974.

---

[1]. J. G. A g a r d h, in Alg. Syst. 3, p. 60, refers it to *Porphyra (Diploderma) miniata* (L y n g b.), and he records this species as monostromatic.

f. *typica*.
Descr. Porphyra laciniata Thur. in Le Jol. Liste Alg. Cherb. p. 100.
Fig.   „   „   Harv. Phyc. Brit. t. 92.
Exsicc.   „   „   Aresch. Alg. Scand. exsicc. Nr. 116, 312.
  „   „   var. elongata Aresch l. c. Nr. 117.
  „   vulgaris Aresch. l. c. Nr. 261.

f. *umbilicalis* L. (Kleen.)
Nordl. Alg. p. 23; Ulva umbilicalis L. Spec. Pl. 2, p. 1163.
Descr. Ulva umbilicalis Lyngb. Hydr. Dan. p. 28.
Exsicc. Porphyra laciniata f. *b*. Aresch. Alg. Scand. exsicc. Nr. 260.
Syn. Ulva umbilicalis Gunn. Fl. Norv. 2, p. 121.
  „   „   Wg. Fl. Lapp. p. 506; excl. var.

This species is also at East-Finmarken much varying, appearing in a rather large number of forms. I have not succeeded in drawing any limits between them, with exception of f. *umbilicalis*, which is a well differentiated form. The specimens distributed in A r e s c h o u g Alg. Scand. exsicc. l. c. will show some of the forms that I mean by f. *typica*, or have referred to this form. It varies as to the colour by dried specimens between light flesh-coloured and amethystine. The thickness of the frond is generally 30—40 µ, but I have collected specimens which were, at the middle, 60 µ thick. The difference seems chiefly to be founded upon the conditions at the places where the plant is growing. In the inner part of deep bays it becomes seldom lobed, but here it often reaches a considerable size. Thus I have seen specimens at Russemark (Porsangerfjord) in West-Finmarken, being in general perfectly simple and attaining a length of 2 metre by a breadth of 0.5 m. and more.

The typical form is litoral or sublitoral. In the former case it grows mostly scattered, attached to rocks or other algæ, as *Halosaccion ramentaceum*, *Dumontia filiformis*, *Rhodymenia palmata* etc. In the latter case I have only met with it fastened to other algæ, for inst. *Lithothamnia*, *Ptilota* and *Laminaria*. It descends to a depth of about 8 fathoms. The form *umbilicalis* is always litoral and fastened to rocks or stones near high-water mark. It is sometimes gregarious, though never in as large number as farther south, and it becomes best developed on exposed places, but appears also in rather sheltered localities. The typical form, on the other hand, thrives best on protected places. Specimens with reproductive organs have been taken at the end of June, in July and August.

Distribution: Common along the whole coast; at several places in rather large number.

Porphyra abyssicola Kjellm.
N. Ish. Algfl. p. 240.
Descr. Porphyra abyssicola Kjellm. l. c.
Fig. „ „ „ „ t. 17, fig. 4 et t. 18, fig. 10—11.
Syn. Porphyra m'niata Kleen, Nordl. Alg. p. 23, sec. Kjellm. l. c.

Also this species is somewhat variable. With reference to the form of the frond it resembles *Diploderma amplissimum* f. *typica*, but never as much folded as that species. I have even seen specimens which were quite smooth. The largest one I have collected had a length of 28 cm. by 12 cm. in breadth in its broadest part. Yet it is generally much smaller, and I have not seldom met with individuals bearing reproductive organs, which were only 3 cm. long. Sterile individuals are rather difficult to distinguish from certain forms of *P. laciniata*.

The plant is sublitoral, appearing on a depth of 5—15 fathoms, most commonly attached to other algae, as *Ptilota pectinata*, *Euthora cristata*, *Rhodophyllis dichotoma*, *Odonthalia dentata* and *Desmarestia aculeata*. It has only been found on open coast. Specimens with reproductive organs have been collected in the later half of June, in July and in the earlier half of August.

Distribution: Found at Kjöllefjord and Sværholt, scanty; Mehavn, rather scarce, Berlevaag and Vardö, cast on shore in a few individuals. Probably it appears scattered along the whole coast.

Gen. **Bangia** (Lyngb.) Kütz.
Phyc. gener. p. 248; Lyngb. Hydr. Dan. p. 82; lim. mut.

Bangia fuscopurpurea (Dillw.) Lyngb.
. c. p. 83; Conferva fuscopurpurea Dillw. Brit. Conf. p. 92.
Descr. Bangia fuscopurpurea Hauck, Meeresalg. p. 22.
  " atropurpurea β fuscopurpurea J. G. Ag Alg. Syst. 3, p. 36.
Fig. "   "   "   " t. 1, fig. 34—39.
  " fuscopurpurea Harv. Phyc. Brit. t. 96.
  "   " Kütz. Tab. Phyc. 3, t. 29.
Exsicc. " " Aresch. Alg. Scand. exsicc. Nr. 118.
Syn. Conferva atropurpurea Wg. Fl. Lapp. p. 515.

Besides the typical form of this species I have collected another one, which has a chlorophyll-green colour. Cp. Schmitz, Chromatoph. p. 3. It is reduced in size, the threads thin and somewhat curled, or often subclavate, forming rather interwoven strata on rocks near high-water mark, on exposed places. Only barren specimens have been found.

The typical form is also litoral, and grows on rocks in the lower part of the zone. I have only met with it in much exposed localities. The length of the threads is generally 2—5 cm. It is furnished with sporocarps and antheridia in the middle of August.

Distribution: The typical form found at Sværholt, common and abundant in the neighbourhood of «Klubben» and at «Vestersiden»; Vardö, local but pretty plentiful. The chlorophyll green form found at Vardö, local and scarce, and at Bugönæs in Sydvaranger, rare.

Bangia crispa Lyngb.
Hydr. Dan. p. 82.
Descr. Bangia crispa J. G. Ag. Alg. Syst. 3, p. 33.
Fig. "   "   "   " t. t. fig. 18—22.

Fig. Bangia crispa Lyngb. l. c. t. 24.
    „   „   Kütz. Tab. Phyc. 3, t. 28.
Exsicc. „   „   Aresch. Alg. Scand. exsicc. Nr. 18.

By the kindness of J. G. Agardh I have had the opportunity of examining an authentic specimen of this species from Bohuslän. The Finmarkian specimens coincide fully with that one, only smaller and a little thinner. Among the quoted figures it most nearly resembles Kützing's *B. crispa* Tab. Phyc. 3, t. 28, fig. a.

The plant is litoral, occurring on rocks near high-water mark, on exposed coast, together with *Calothrix scopulorum*.

Distribution: Only found at Kjelmö in Sydvaranger, rare.

Bangia virescens nob.

B. rupicola, luteo-virens; fllis cylindraceis, simplicibus articulatis, 12—30 μ crassis, dense intricatis atque crispis, arcticulis æqualibus ad triplo brevioribus. Tab. 2, fig. 2—9.

The species forms rather thick, uniform and sometimes extensive strata on rocks between tides, mostly at high-water mark in exposed localities. The surface is a little rough or undulate-lacunosed. It has a yellow-green colour, and its habit is rather that of an *Urospora* than a *Bangia*. It also sometimes grows alternating or mixed with *Urospora penicilliformis*. The thickness of the threads varies between 12 and 30 μ, most commonly about 20. They are so densely interwoven that pretty large parts of the layer may be easely removed from the rock with a knife.

The plant seems to be dioecious. But I am uncertain whether the organs figured on t. 2, fig. 7—9 really are sporocarps and antheridia. It has been collected with these organs at East Finmarken in July and at West-Finmarken at the end of May. It seems to disappear in August

Distribution; Pretty common and rather plentiful almost all along the unsheltered part of the coast. I have seen it at Sværholt, Kjöllefjord, Mehavn, Omgang, Kiberg, Ekkerö and Bugönæs.

Ser. Fucoideæ (Ag.) J. G. Ag.
Alg. Med. p. 24; Ag. Syst. Alg. p. XXXV; lim. mut.

Fam. Fucaceæ (Ag.) J. G. Ag.
Spec. Alg. 1, p. 180; Ag. Syst. Alg. p. XXXVII; lim. mut.

Gen. Halidrys (Lyngb.) Grev.
Alg. Brit p. XXXIV; Lyngb. Hydr. Dan. p. 37; lim. mut.

Halidrys siliquosa (L.) Lyngb.

l. c. Fucus siliquosus L. Spec. Plant. 2, p. 1160.
Descr.. Halidrys siliquosa J. G. Ag. Spec. Alg 1, p. 236.
Fig. „ „ Harv. Phyc. Brit. t. 66.
Exsicc. „ „ Aresch. Alg. Scand. exsicc. Nr. 151.
  Syn. Fucus siliquosus Gunn. Fl. Norv. 1, p. 83.
    „   „   Wg. Fl. Lapp. p. 498.
  Halidrys siliquosa Aresch. Phyc. Scand. p. 253.

According to Areschoug and Wahlenberg, this species occurs at the coast of Finmarken, but I do not know whether the statements refer to East- or West-Finmarken, or perhaps only to the northern part of the present Tromsö amt, which formerly belonged to Finmarken. I never met with it myself attached, neither at West- nor at East-Finmarken. But at Sværholt I found some vigorous specimens floating close to the shore.

Distribution: Unknown to me, and it may be very doubtful whether it belongs to the Flora of East-Finmarken. Loose specimens found at Svärholt.

Gen. Ozothallia Desne et Thur.
Rech. Fuc. p. 13.

Ozothallia nodosa (L.) Dcsne et Thur.
l. c. Fucus nodosus L. Spec. Plant. 2, p. 1159.
Descr. Fucodium nodosum J. G. Ag. Spec. Alg. 1, p. 206.
Fig. Fucus nodosus Harv. Phyc. Brit. t. 158.
Exsicc. Halicoccus nodosus Aresch. Alg Scand. exsicc. Nr. 51.
  Syn. Fucus nodosus Fl. Dan. t. 146.
  „   „   Gunn. Fl. Norv. 1, p. 33.
  „   „   Wg. Fl. Lapp. p. 499.
  Halidrys nodosa Lyngb. Hydr. Dan. p. 37.
  „   „   Sommerf. in Act. Nidros. p. 51.
  Ascophyllum nodosum Gobi, Algefl. Weiss. Meer. p. 52.
  Halicoccus nodosus Kleen, Nordl. Alg. p. 31.

Chiefly a litoral alga, occupying a broad border mostly in the middle part of the zone. In the inner part of some of the greater bays, for inst. Jarfjord, it descends a little below low-water mark. The plant is vigorously developed, attaining a length of 1.5 m. and more. It bears plenty of receptacles in July. The spores are generally ripe in the middle of the month. Almost all the specimens I have seen in August, even in the beginning of the month, were sterile.

Distribution: Common and in great abundance everywhere.

Gen. **Fucus** (Tourn.) Dcsne et Thur.
Tech. Fuc. p. 13; Tourn. Inst. Herb. 3, p. 565; char. mut.

Fucus serratus L.
Spec. Plant. 2, p. 1158.

f. *grandifrons* Kjellm.
N. Isb. Algfl. p. 245.
Descr. Fucus serratus f. grandifrons Kjellm. l. c

f. *typica* Kjellm.
l. c.
Descr. Fucus serratus f. typica Kjellm. l. c.
Fig. „   „   Harv. Phyc. Brit t. 47.
Exsicc. „   „   Aresch. Alg. Scand. exsicc. Nr. 55.

f. *angusta* Kjellm.
l. c.

Descr. Fucus serratus f. angusta Kjellm. l. c.
   Syn. Fucus serratus Gunn. Fl. Norv. 1, p. 28.
      „   „   Wg. Fl. Lapp. p. 483.
      „   „   Sommerf. in Acta Nidros. p. 50.

Besides the above quoted form, I suppose that also other forms of this species are to be found on the coast of East-Finmarken.[1] The plant often bears air-bladders in the upper part of the thallom (f. *typica* and f. *vadorum*). They are of indefinite shape, mostly much more long than broad, 0.5—7 cm. in length.

The species is litoral, occupying a rather broad border in the lower part of the zone, or sublitoral, descending a few feet below low-water mark (espicially f. *grandifrons*). It appears in much exposed as well as in sheltered places, but, as far as I know, it does not penetrate to the inner end of the greater bays.

Distribution: Common and in great abundance everywhere except in the inner part of the deep fjords.

Fucus vesiculosus L.
   Spec. Plant. 2, p. 1158.
   f. *vadorum* Aresch.
      Fuc. et Pycnoph. p. 102.
Descr. Fucus vesiculosus β vadorum Aresch. l. c.
      „   „   f. vadorum Kleen, Nordl. Alg. p. 26.
   f. *typica*.
Descr. Fucus vesiculosus α rupincola Aresch. l. c.
      „   „   sens. strict. Kleen, l. c.
Fig.   „   „   Harv. Phyc. Brit. t. 204.
Exsicc.   „   „   Aresch. Alg. Scand. exsicc. No. 53.
   f. *angustifrons* Gobi.
      Algenfl. Weiss. Meer. p. 53.

---

[1]. As I have lost the greatest part of my collections of *Fucaceæ* and *Alaria* from Finmarken, my remarks on the species and forms and their distribution are founded on the small rest of the collections brought home, and a number of notes.

Descr. Fucus vesiculosus f. pseudoceranoides Kleen, l. c. p. 27.

    f. *turgida* Kjellm.
    N. Ish. Algfl. p. 248.
Descr. Fucus vesiculosus f. turgida Kjellm. l. c.

    f. *sphærocarpa* J. G. Ag.
    Grönl. Lam. och Fuc. p. 29.
Descr. Fucus vesiculosus ♂ sphærocarpus Kleen, l. c. p. 28.

    f. *subfusiformis* Kjellm.
    Skand. Algfl.
Descr. Fucus vesiculosus f. subfusiformis Kjellm. l. c.
    Syn. Fucus vesiculosus Gunn. Fl. Norv. 1, p. 28.
         „   „   Wg. Fl. Lapp. p. 490; excl. var.
         „   divaricatus Gunn. Fl. Norv. 2, p. 143.

Of the forms quoted above, f. *typica* and f. *turgida* are the most common, but f. *vadorum* and f. *angustifrons* are also pretty common at some places. The plant often bears, in the upper and barren segments, long and rather narrow air-bladders like those by the preceding species, and on the same individual air-bladders of the common form besides. It is litoral, growing in the upper as well as in the lower part of the zone, and sometimes descending a little below low-water mark. It bears receptacles in June, July and August.

Distribution: Common and very abundant everywhere.

Fucus spiralis L.
Spec. Plant. 2, p. 1159.

    f. *borealis* Kjellm.
    N. Ish. Algfl. p. 252.
Descr. Fucus spiralis f. borealis Kjellm. l. c.
    Syn. Fucus Areschougii Kjellm. mscr.

Litoral, mostly growing at or a little below high-water, forming a narrow girdle, or often somewhat scattered. It appears to prefer open coast. Specimens bearing receptacles have been collected in June, July and August.

Distribution: Pretty common almost all along the open

part of the coast, as at Sværholt (plentiful), Berlevaag, Vardö and Ekkerö (rather numerous).

Fucus inflatus L; Vahl.
Fl. Dan. t. 1127; L Fl. Lapp. p. 351. Cfr. Fosl. in Tromsö Mus. Aarsh. IX, p. 109.

f. *typica*.
Descr. Fucus furcatus Aresch. Fuc. et Pycnoph. p. 107.
Exsicc. „   „   „   Alg Scand exsicc. Nr. 401.

f. *latifrons* Fosl. mscr.
Fucus inflatus Fl. Dan. l. c.

This species is rather variable, and may perhaps include other forms than the above mentioned ones, which ought to be kept distinct. At several places I met with a form *pygmæa* on rocks at high-water mark. It is only 3—4 cm. long bearing richly receptacles, but as yet I do not know whether it may be regarded only a stunted form produced by unfavourable conditions of life. I have, on the contrary, seen specimens most nearly related to the typical form bearing receptacles even 11 cm. in length. The form *latifrons* corresponds with f. *grandifrons* of *F. serratus* and f. *vadorum* of *F. vesiculosus*. It generally bears air-bladders of a lengthened shape until 8 cm. long. The typical form also is provided with such ones, though more seldom.

The present plant is litoral, mostly occurring in the lower part of the zone, and at several places it forms a rather broad girdle, at others growing in company with *F. vesiculosus* or *F. serratus*. Although it appears in great abundance at most places along the unsheltered part of the coast, the number of individuals seem in general to be less than at West-Finmarken. It bears receptacles in June and July (f. *typica*), and in the first part of August (f. *vadorum*). The latter grows farther down than the typical form, at extreme low-water mark, or perhaps descending into the sublitoral zone. It seems to prefer sheltered localities.

Distribution: Common and very abundant along the open coast, and penetrating pretty far into the deep fjords. The form *latifrons* found at Vardö (washed ashore) and at Sværholt, pretty common.

Fucus miclonensis De la Pyl.
Fl. Terre neuve p. 90.
Descr. Fucus miclonensis J. G. Ag. Spetsb. Alg. Till. p. 39.
 „ distichus var. miclonensis Kleen, Nordl. Alg. p. 30.
Fig. „ miclonensis Kjellm. N. Isb. Algfl. t. 19, fig. 1—2.

I met with some few specimens of this alga, growing in rock-pools in the upper part of the litoral zone. They coincide well with specimens from Greenland, determined by J. G. Agardh, bearing receptacles in July.

Distribution: Only found at Mehavn, scarce. Probably more commonly spread.

Fucus linearis Fl. Dan.
t. 351.
Descr. Fucus linearis J. G. Ag. Spetsb. Alg. Till. p. 39.
Fig. „ „ Fl. Dan. l. c.

The specimens that I have referred to this species agree well with specimens from Greenland, determined by J. G. Agardh. They grew in rock-pools in the upper part of the litoral region. Specimens bearing receptacles have been collected in July.

Distribution: Found at Mehavn and Vardö, scarce.

Fucus filiformis Gmel.
Hist. Fuc. p. 72.

f. *Gmelini* J. G. Ag.
Spetsb. Alg. Till. p. 38.
Descr. Fucus filiformis α. Gmelini J. G. Ag. l. c.
Fig. „ „ f. „ Kjellm. N. Isb. Algfl. t. 19, fig. 3.

f. *Pylaisæi* J. G. Ag.
Spetsb. Alg. Till. p. 38.

Descr. Fucus filiformis *b.* Pylaisæi J. G. Ag. l. c.
Fig. „ linearis Kütz. Tab. Phyc. 10, t. 15.
Exsicc. „ distichus Aresch. Alg. Scand. exsicc. Nr. 201.
  Syn. Fucus distichus Aresch. Phyc. Scand. p. 257.

I have referred to the present species forms which by others are considered more nearly related to *F. inflatus*, the species taken in the same sense as described by J. G. A g a r d h. The plant is litoral, always occurring in rock-pools in the upper part of the zone, on open coasts as well as sheltered ones. It bears receptacles in June and the earlier half of July.

Distribution: Common and plentiful almost everywhere.

Fucus distichus L.
Syst. Nat. Ed. 12, 2, p. 716.

f. *robustior* J. G. Ag.
Spetsb. Alg. Till. p. 37.

Descr. Fucus distichus *a.* robustior J. G. Ag. l. c.
Fig. „ „ Kütz. Tab. Phyc. 10, t. 15, fig. d.

f. *tenuior* J. G. Ag.
l. c.

Descr. Fucus distichus *b.* tenuior J. G. Ag. l. c.
Fig. „ „ Turn. Hist. Fuc. t. 4.

Litoral, growing in rock-pools in the upper part of the region. Specimens bearing receptacles have been collected in the first part of July.

Distribution: Found at Mehavn (f. *robustior* and f. *tenuior*), and at Berlevaag and Sværholt, scarce.[1]

Gen. **Pelvetia** Desne et Thur.
Rech. Fuc. p. 12.

---

[1]. I found some barren specimens of a *Fucus* which reminds of *F. Fucci*. Typical specimens of this species I have seen in rather large number at West-Finmarken, bearing receptacles in the middle of August.

Pelvetia canaliculata (L.) Desne et Thur.
l. c. Fucus canaliculatus L. Syst. Nat. Ed. 12, 2, p. 716.
Descr. Fucodium canaliculatum J. G. Ag. Spec. Alg. 1, p. 204.
Fig. Fucus canaliculatus Harv. Phyc. Brit. t. 229.
Exsicc. „ „ Aresch. Alg. Scand. exsicc. No. 202.
Pelvetia canaliculata Hauck et Richt. Phyc. univ. No. 216.
Syn. Fucus excisus Gunn. Fl. Norv. 1, p. 96.
„ „ Fl. Dan. t. 214.
„ canaliculatus Wg. Fl. Lapp. p. 495.

This species always grows in the uppermost part of the litoral zone, at high-water mark, or sometimes even a little higher up. At East-Finmarken it appears scattered, or perhaps more often gregarious in a number of individuals, though never in so large number as farther south. Specimens with receptacles have been collected in July and August.

Distribution: Scattered and scarce at Sværholt, Kjöllefjord, Mehavn, Berlevaag and Syltefjord; Vardö, pretty plentiful but local.

Fam. **Tilopterideæ** Thur.
in Le Jol. Liste Alg. Cherb. p. 16.

Gen. **Haplospora** Kjellm.
Scand. Ect. och Tilopt. p. 16.

Haplospora globosa Kjellm.
l. c. p. 5.
Descr. Haplospora globosa Kjellm. l. c.
Fig. „ „ „ „ t. 1, fig. 1.

A couple of specimens, bearing reproductive organs, have been collected in the upper part of the sublitoral region, on a depth of 5—6 fathoms.

Distribution: Only found at Kjöllefjord, very rare.

Fam. **Laminariaceæ** (Ag.) Thur.

in Le Jol. Liste Alg. Cherb. p. 15; Ag. Syst. Alg. p. XXXVI; lim. mut.

Gen. **Alaria** Grev.
Alg. Brit. p. XXXIX.

Alaria esculenta (L.) Grev.

l. c. p. 25; Fucus esculentus L. Mant. 1, p. 135.

f. *pinnata* (Gunn.) Fosl.

Krit. fortegn. p. '113; Fucus pinnatus Gunn. Fl. Norv. 1, p. .

Descr. Alaria musæfolia J. G. Ag. Grönl. Lamin. och Fuc. p. 23.

Fig. Laminaria esculenta var. platyphylla De la Pyl. Prodr. Terr. neuve, t. 9, fig. D.

Syn. Fucus esculentus Wg. Fl. Lapp. p. 494.

Alaria esculenta f. musœfolia Kjellm. N. Ish. Algfl. p. 265.

The form of this species, which occurs at the coast of East-Finmarken, seems to be scarce. I have only seen a few specimens. Perhaps it is more commonly spread.

Distribution: Unknown to me. I have met with it at Sværholt and Mehavn.

Alaria Pylaii (De la Pyl.) J. G. Ag.

Grönl. Lam. och Fuc. p. 24; Laminaria Pylaii De la Pyl. Fl. Terre neuve p. 29.

Descr. Alaria Pylaii J. G. Ag. l. c.

Litoral and sublitoral. It often grows in rock-pools in the lower part of the litoral zone, but here it mostly gets rather dwarfed. It is best developed in the upper part of the sublitoral zone, on a depth of 1—8 fathoms, and here I have seen specimens which had a length of 1 m. and more. A young specimen taken on a depth of 5—8 fathoms has a proportionally broad lamina.[1] The stipe of it is 8 cm. long, bearing a few very young (2 mm. long) sporophylls. The

---

[1]. The elder specimens I collected are lost, and I have not exact measure of them.

lamina is ovate-lanceolate, 40 cm. long and 8 cm. broad in the broadest part (dried spec.), with rounded and a little decurrent base.

The species in question appears on open and exposed coasts as well as in more sheltered localities, and it even enters pretty far into the deeper bays.

Distribution: Common and plentiful all along the coast.

A l a r i a m e m b r a n a c e a J. G. Ag.
Grönl. Lam. och Fuc. p. 26.
Descr. Alaria membranacea J. G. Ag. l. c.
Syn. Orgyia pinnata Gobi, Algenfl. Weiss. Meer. p. 77.

I think this species to be so nearly related to the following one, that any limit hardly may be drawn between them. It is no doubt the most common *Alaria* along the unsheltered part of the coast. It is here vigorous and very luxuriant, reaching considerable dimensions. I shall give the measurments of some of the largest specimens I collected.

Total-length.	Stipes.	Rhachis.	Lamina.	
			Length.	Breadth.
3.72 m.	0.18 m.	0.20 m.	3.34 m.	0.18 m.
2.87	0.13	0.18	2.56	0.31
2.90	0.11	0.17	2.62	0.29
4.11	0.25	0.20	3.66	0.19

A young specimen collected together with the above mentioned ones has a remarkably narrow lamina, reminding of *A. linearis* S t r ö m f. The stipe of it is 8.5 cm. long and bears a few very young (1—5 mm. long) sporophylls. The lamina is lanceolate-linear, 115 cm. long and 4.3 cm. broad in the broadest part (dried spec.) with angustated base.

On an iron buoy at Berlevaag, laid out in July—August 1885, and put on shore for cleaning in July 1887, I found a smaller specimen, the stem of which had a thickness of nearly 1 cm., showing in a transverse section two concentric rings. One of these rings, the outer, is somewhat indistinct,

Probably these rings indicate the number of years the plant has existed, answering to the space of time the buoy has been in the sea. The rhachis was provided with sporophylls and showing scars of such organs that had fallen off.

The species occurs in the upper part of the sublitoral zone, on a depth of 1—(10?) fathoms, and becomes best developed in rocky and much exposed localities. Specimens with zoosporangia have been collected in July.

Distribution: Common and abundant at least along the open part of the coast from Sværholt to Kiberg in the neighbourhood of Vardö.

Alaria grandifolia J. G. Ag.
Grönl. Lam. och. Fuc. p. 26.
Descr Alaria grandifolia J. G. Ag. l. c.
„   „   Kjellm. Spetsb. Thall. 2, p. 10.

I found at Kiberg a specimen of an *Alaria*, which probably belongs to this species. The stem (including rhachis) had a length of 1.5 m. and a diameter of 2 cm. Of the lamina only a small portion was left, the costa had a breadth of 17 mm. Judging from other fragments I suppose this species to occur all along the open coast. Thus at Mehavn and Kjöllefjord I got fragments of laminæ having a breadth of until 50 cm , and fragments of very coarse and long stems.

Distribution: Common and plentiful (?) along the open coast.[1]

---

[1]. I also met with other forms. But as before mentioned, I have lost the greatest part of my collections of *Alaria* from East- as well as from West-Finmarken, and the examination of the specimens when collected, and the notes from my excursions are too little particular to record these f·rms here, espicially in the case of a genus with so feeble marked forms as *Alaria*.

At a sunken rock about two (engl.) mi'es from the outer side of Kjelmö in Sydvaranger I sow on a depth of 2—3 fathoms an *Alaria* which reminds of *A. Pylaii*, but the specimens had a remarkably nar-

Gen. Phyllaria Le Jol.
Exam. p. 72.

Phyllaria dermatodea (De la Pyl.) Le Jol.

l. c. Laminaria dermatodea De la Pyl. Prod. Terre neuve, p. 180.
Descr. Saccorhiza dermatodea Farl. New. Engl. Alg. p. 95.
      Phyllaria   „   Kjellm. N. Ish. Algfl. p. 278.
Exsicc. Laminaria lorea Aresch. Alg. Scand. exsicc. No. 213.
    Syn. Saccorhiza dermatodea Aresch. Obs. Phyc. 3, p. 11.

Ph. dermatodea and *Ph. lorea* (Bory) recently have been kept distinct by Kjellman (l. c.). The one, *Ph. lorea*, according to Kjellman, has only been found at the west and north coasts of Spitzbergen and the west coast of Novaya Zemlya. The former has a wide dispersion.

Also at the coast of Finmarken two forms of *Phyllaria* appear. But at present I am unable to ascertain whether these forms are to be regarded as distinct species or, as I am most inclined to think, only little differentiated forms of one and the same species. The one has a proportionally short stipe, linear lanceolate lamina with numerous cryptostomata. It attains a length of 2 m and more. I call it f. *lanceolata*. The following are the measures of some of the larger specimens.

Stipes' length.	Length of lamina.	Breadth of lamina.
19 cm.	135 cm.	6 cm.
18	142	5
15.5	124	8.5
12.5	107	4.5
21.5	138	5.5

I also have seen a pretty large number of young specimens with a short stipe, linear or lanceolate lamina, closely resembling *Ph. lorea* Kjellm. l. c. t. 24, fig. 1—2. The

---

row lamina. I did not succeed to get hold of any. It may perhaps have been *A. linearis* Strömf. or another species not formerly known from Finmarken.

colour is yellowish brown by dried specimens. Thus in outward appearance they agree fully with young plants of *Ph. lorea* as described by Kjellman l. c. But they are, as far as I am able to judge, young plants of the above mentioned f. *lanceolata*. I shall give the measures of some of them.

Stipes' length.	Length of lamina.	Breadth of lamina.
5 cm.	44 cm.	2.3 cm.
2	18	1
1	14.5	0.8
2	25	1.3
2	19	1
3.5	17	1.8
2.5	20	1
2.3	12	0.6
0.5	11	0.1
0.5	7.5	0.2

The form *lanceolata* is the most common one, and young as well as elder specimens occur plentifully on much exposed places along the open coast of East-Finmarken, for inst. Omgang, Havningberg, Vardö and Kiberg.

The other form, which I call f. *oblonga*, has an oblong, oblong-lanceolate or ovate-lanceolate lamina, cryptostomata commonly fewer and the colour a little darker than by the preceding one, especially the stipe and the lower part of the lamina. The stipe is more or less distinctly marked from the lamina. The following measures show the proportions by young and elder specimens.

Stipes' length.	Length of lamina.	Breadth of lamina.
13 cm.	28 cm.	13 cm.
11	35.5	15
12	25	9
3	6	2.7
6	6.5	3.3

Stipes' length.   Length of lamina.   Breadth of lamina.
0.5 cm.   2 cm.   1 cm.

Unfortunately, I have not examined the structure by living specimens, and having alcohol-materials only of f. *oblonga*, I cannot at present decide the mutual connection in this respect between the two forms and their relation to *Ph. lorea* (B o r y) K j e l l m.

Ph. dermatodea is a pelagic alga, best developed on open coasts. In much exposed places it becomes very narrow (f. *lanceolata*), analogous to other *Laminariaceæ*, for inst. *L. saccharina*, but contrary to several other algæ, as *Odonthalia dentata*, *Rhodophyllis dichotoma*, *Phyllitis fascia*, which get narrow in much sheltered localities, or in the interior of deep bays. In less exposed places, on the other hand, or in deeper water, *Ph. dermatodea* becomes shorter, with proportionally much broader lamina, and here it often also gets a little darker (f. *oblonga*). The former grows in the uppermost part of the sublitoral zone, and sometimes also in rockpools in the lower part of the litoral zone, the latter only in the sublitoral zone and generally on a depth of 5—10 fathoms. Specimens collected in June, July and the earlier half of August were sterile.

Distribution: Common and rather plentiful all along the open coast, at some places abundant, and entering pretty far into the deeper bays.

Gen. Laminaria (Lamour.) J. G. Ag.
Lam. p. 7; Lamour. Ess. p. 40; char. mut.

L a m i n a r i a s a c c h a r i n a (L.) Lamour.
Essai p. 32; Fucus saccharinus L. Spec. plant. 2, p. 1161.

f. *linearis* J. G. Ag.
Lam. p. 12.

Descr. Laminaria saccharina α linearis J. G. Ag. l. c.
      „   „   f. linearis Fosl. Lam. Norw. p. 95.

Fig. Fucus saccharinus Fl. Dan. t. 416.

f. *oblonga* J. G. Ag.
Lam. p. 12.
Descr. Laminaria saccharina *b.* oblonga J. G. Ag. l. c.
„ „ f. oblonga Fosl. Lam. Norw. p. 96.

f. *longissima* (Gunn.) Fosl.
Lam. Norw. p. 91; Ulva longissima Gunn. Fl. Norv. 2, p. 128.
Descr. Laminaria saccharina f. grandifolia Kjellm. N. Ish. Algfl. p. 287.
„ „ f. longissima Fosl. Lam. Norw. p. 96.
Fig. „ „ f. grandifolia Kjellm. l. c. t. 25, fig. 7.

f. *borealis* Fosl.
Lam. Norw. p. 91.
Descr. Laminaria saccharina f. latissima Kjellm. N. Ish. Algfl. p. 287.
„ „ f. borealis Fosl. Lam. Norw. p. 97.

f. *Agardhii* Kjellm. (Fosl.)
Lam. Norw. p. 91; Laminaria Agardhii Kjellm. Spetsb. Thall. 2, p. 18.
Descr. Laminaria caperata J. G. Ag. Lam. p. 13.
„ Agardhii Kjellm. Spetsb. Thall. 2, p. 18 et N. I. Algfl. 291.
Fig. „ „ „ „ „ t. 1, fig. 2—3.
Syn. Ulva latissima Gunn. Fl. Norv. 1, p. 52.
Fucus saccharinus Gunn. l. c.
Ulva maxima Gunn. l. c. 2, p. 127.
Laminaria caperata Kleen, Nordl. Alg. p. 32.

As stated in Lam. Norw. l. c., a form of this species occurs at East-Finmarken, which, as far as I am able to judge, must be referred to *L. Agardhii* Kjellm., common at the coasts of Spitzbergen, Novaya Zemlya and probably also in the White Sea. It is on the other hand so nearly related to certain forms of *L. saccharina*, that I am unable to draw any limit. According to Kjellman it is different from that species mainly by the wanting of muciferous lacunæ. The lacunæ are in general pretty common in the lamina by Scandinavian specimens of *L. saccharina*, sometimes very large, sometimes small, but not seldom quite wanting. As far as I have seen, it depends on the localities and conditions where the plant grows. Cp. Fosl. l. c. p. 94.

The most common form of the species is f. *linearis*. In much exposed localities, for inst. Omgang, it becomes very luxuriant, attaining a length of 4 metre and more. It grows in the limit between the litoral and the sublitoral regions, and descends to a depth of about 2—3 fathoms. Here it is succeeded by f. *oblonga*, which descends to a depth of about 8 fathoms. The other forms generally occur farther down, up to about 20 fathoms. A reduced form that appears in rock-pools between tides I have referred to f. *oblonga*. It sometimes is reniform with truncated top.

The plant seems to develop its reproductive organs in the winter or early in the spring. In the summer specimens have often been met with bearing fragments of an earlier lamina even as late as in the later part of July.

Distribution: Common and abundant almost everywhere. The form *linearis* only along the unsheltered and exposed part of the coast; f. *oblonga* in exposed as well as in somewhat sheltered places; f. *longissima* and f. *borealis* enter the inner end of the deep bays; f. *Agardhii* only found some few times on open coast.

Laminaria nigripes J. G. Ag.

Spetsb. Alg. Till. p. 29.

Descr. Laminaria nigripes J. G. Ag. l. c.
   „ „ „ Grönl. Lam. och Fuc. p. 17.
   „ „ Kjellm. N. Ish. Algfl. p. 295.
Fig. „ „ „ t. 25, fig. 8—10.
Syn. Laminaria nigripes Fosl. Lam. Norw. p. 58.

I have but rarely met with this species washed ashore. It probably grows in the upper part of the sublitoral region. But I suppose it to be more commonly spread along the open part of the coast. The specimens I have seen are most nearly to be related to f. *oblonga* Kjellm.

Distribution: Found at Berlevaag, a few specimens, and at Vardö, a single specimen.

Laminaria Gunneri Fosl.
Lam. Norw. p. 54.
Descr. Laminaria Gunneri Fosl. l. c.
Fig   „   „   „   „ t. 2.

I have been uncertain whether this species ought to be kept distinct, or only to be regarded as a form of *L. nigripes*. I have latterly got a number of other and better conserved specimens than I had by the description of this plant. I then quoted the colour to be very dark, almost black, and the lamina inpellucid. This appears now chiefly to be founded thereon, that the specimens probably have lain on the beach for some time. The colour really is only a little darker than by *L. nigripes*.

After a careful examination of the materials I have at my disposal I find, however, that the plant in question must be considered a distinct species. It is smaller than *L. nigripes*. The length is varying between 30 and 60 cm. By 14 specimens the stipe has a length of 7—22 cm., and the length of the lamina by 26 specimens is 20—40 cm.[1] *L. nigripes* is commonly much larger and a more vigorous plant. Of this plant I have collected specimens, the lamina of which has a length of 130 cm. (a part of the stipe is wanting), and its consistency is less solid than by *L. Gunneri*. By a transverse section of the middle part of the lamina of *L. Gunneri*, the cells of the intermediate layer are more equal in size in the greater part of the layer, angular or rounded-angular, not seldom squarish, with thick walls and often ranged in more or less regular longitudinal series. The named layer is more or less sharply defined from the middle one, and the latter is thicker in proportion to the intermediate layer than by *L. nigripes*. By a similar section of *L. nigripes* the cells of the intermediate layer are more irregular with regard to the form as well as the size, with thinner walls, and they are

---

[1]. 12 specimens are wanting the lower part of the stipe.

largest near the middle layer. Cp. Kjellm. l. c. t. 25, fig. 10. The muciferous lacunæ seem in general to be more numerous by *L. Gunneri* and often also larger, especially in the lamina, than by *L. nigripes*.

The sorus is never developed to the base of the lamina such as by *L. nigripes*. Cp. Kjellm. l. c. p. 297. A moon-shaped, 5—8 cm. high part of the base is always barren. From here it forms a broad girdle, 10—30 cm. upwards, commonly 15—25 cm., and sometimes extending to the top of the segments.

L. Gunneri appears to live in the upper part of the sublitoral region, though probably farther down than *L. nigripes*, because the former has been found only after heavy winter-gales, but the latter also washed ashore in the summer. The plant is fastened to stones, or more often to dying stems of *Alaria* and *Laminaria hyperborea*. Most of the specimens I got are said to have been collected in February and March, and these bear zoospores. A few that have been taken in November are sterile.

Distribution: Only found at Berlevaag, probably rather scarce.

Laminaria hyperborea (Gunn.) Fosl.

Lam. Norw. p. 42; Fucus hyperboreus Gunn. Fl. Norv. 1, p. 34.

f. *typica* Fosl.

Bidr. p. 15.

Descr. Laminaria Cloustoni Le Jol. Exam. p. 56.
       Hafgygia   „   Aresch. Obs. Phyc. 4, p. 1.
       Laminaria hyperborea Fosl. Lam. Norw. p. 42.

Fig.   „   „   „   „   t. 1, fig. 1—8.
       „   digitata Harv. Phyc. Brit. t. 223, fig. 1.

f. *compressa* Fosl.

Lam. Norw. p. 42.

Descr. Laminaria digitata f. longifolia Fosl. Bidr. p. 19.
       „   hyperborea f. compressa Fosl. Lam. Norw. p. 42.

Fig.   „   „   „   „   „   t. 1, fig. 9.

Syn. Fucus digitatus Wg. Fl. Lapp. p. 492; ex parte.
„   „   Fl. Dan. t. 392.
Laminaria Clustoni Kjellm. N. Ish. Algfl. p. 298.

Sublitoral, occurring in 2—10 fathoms water, or probably descending up to a still greater depth. It is luxuriant and vigorous along the open coast, particularly in much exposed localities. Here the stipe generally has a height of 1.5—2 m. by a diameter in the lower part of 3—5 cm. The lamina has a length of 40—60 cm. But the plant often gets much larger. In deep water or in somewhat sheltered places the stem becomes smaller and the lamina proportionally larger, often with fewer and broader segments. Cp. Fosl. l. c. It enters pretty far into the greater bays but here it does not thrive, getting small and stunted. I do not know when it develops its reproductive organs.

Distribution: The typical form common and very abundant all along the open coast; f. *compressa* only found at Berlevaag, scarce.

Laminaria digitata (L.) Edm.

Fl. Shetl. p. 54, sec. Le Jol. Ex. p. 56; Fucus digitatus L Mant. 134.

f. *valida* Fosl.

Bidr. p. 27.

Descr. Laminaria flexicaulis f. valida Fosl. l. c.
„   digitata f. valida Fosl. Lam. Norw. p. 65.
Fig. „ „ „ „ „ t. 3, fig. 1—4.

f. *grandifolia* Fosl.

Lam. Norw. p. 60.

Descr. Laminaria digitata f. grandifolia Fosl. l. c.

f. *complanata* Kjellm.

Kariska hafv. Algveg. p. 26.

Descr. Laminaria digitata f. complanata Kjellm. l. c. et Alg. Murm. Meer. 38.
Fig. „ „ „ Kjellm. Kar. hafv. Alg. t. 1, 14—18.

f. *genuina* Le Jol.

Exam. p. 59.

Descr. Laminaria flexicaulis a. genuina Le Jol. l. c.
  „   digitata f. typica Fosl. Lam. Norw. . 69.
Fig.   „   „   „   „   „   t. 4 et t. 5, fig. 1.
Exsicc.   „   „   Aresch. Alg. Scand. exsicc. No. 86.

f. *ensifolia* Le Jol.

Exam. p. 57.

Descr. Laminaria flexicaulis d. ensifolia Le Jol. l. c.
  „   digitata f. ensifolia Fosl. Lam. Norw. p. 79.
Fig.   „   „   „   „   „   t. 5, fig. 2—5 et t. 6, 1—9.

f. *stenophylla* Harv.

Phyc. Brit. t. 338.

Descr. Laminaria stenophylla J. G. Ag. Lam. p. 18.
  „   digitata f. stenophylla Fosl. Lam. Norw. p. 74.
Fig.   „   „   var. stenophylla Harv. Phyc. Brit. t. 338.
  „   „   f. stenophylla Fosl. l. c. t. 3, fig. 5—9.
  „   stenophylla Strömf. Isl. Algveg. t. 2, fig. 8.

Syn. Fucus bifurcatus Gunn. Fl. Norv. 1, p. 96.
  Laminaria digitata Kleen, Nordl. Alg. p. 33; ex parte.
  „   „   Kjellm. N. Ish. Algfl. p. 299; excl. var.
  „   flexicaulis Kjellm. l. c. p. 303.
  „   „   Aresch. Obs. Phyc. p. 9.

This is one of the most varying species of the *Laminariaceæ*. The length of full grown specimens is varying between 0.5 and 3.5 m. The variableness is partly founded upon the conditions and localities where the plant grows.

Strömfelt (Isl. Algveg. p. 45) has blamed me that I have misapprehended the form *stenophylla*, and referred to it forms with angustated lamina below, and, therefore, he supposes, I cannot entitle it to rank as a distinct species. He also quotes that he has examined specimens in the Botanical Museum of Upsala, collected at Lödingen in Nordland, and determined by me. I cannot remember having sent algæ to that Museum. In every case f. *stenophylla* does not occur at Lödingen. I know pretty well the marine vegetation there. In Lam. Norw. I have stated that the lamina of f. *genuina* not seldom appears with cuniform base. But f.

stenophylla is distinguished from that one by its dark colour, smoothness and gloss, proportionally feeble and pliable stipe, long and narrow lamina, which is cut up in more or less numerous and narrow segments, and with a cuneate base. In several places along the coast of Norway I have met with a form having the quoted habit and outward appearance, and consequently I have referred it to f. *stenophylla*. The form from Finmarken represented in Lam. Norv. t. 3, fig. 5 has the base of the lamina a little broader, but otherwise fully agreeing with typical *stenophylla*. The consistence of the lamina is more solid than by the other forms except f. *valida*, but the stipe is less solid than by f. *genuina* when it grows in exposed localities. S t r ö m f e l t also points out a difference with regard to the structure. In this respect there is, according to my experience, a pretty large variation by the forms of *L. digitata*. For inst. f. *valida* has not seldom proportionally small cells in the intermediate layer of the lamina, and the consistence as solid as by f. *stenophylla*, the same colour, smoothness and gloss when it grows in certain localities, for inst. Borgevær in Lofoten, and here it is very characteristic. In other localities, however, it is so nearly related to f. *genuina* that no limit hardly may be drawn between them. Other striking examples as to the variation of the outward appearance and sometimes also the structure by the *Laminariæ* afford *L. saccharina* as well as *L. hyperborea*, no doubt greatly dependent on the place af growth. What a difference between *L. saccharina* f. *linearis* with a short stipe, 20—30 cm. in length, a thick, coriaceous and rugose lamina 3.5 m. in length but only 10—12 cm. in breadth, and the form *borealis* growing in enclosed sounds or quiet bays, sometimes with a stipe of nearly 1 m in length, and a thin lamina about 1.5 m. long and nearly the same breadth, with a smooth surface. But every transition is to be found. And so also *L. hyperborea* growing in exposed places on open coasts, having a stipe 2 m. high by a diameter at the base of 4—5 cm., tapering towards the top, and a lamina only 40 cm. long; but in sheltered places a short stipe, often only 30—50 cm. high, almost destitute of cork layer, less solid and proportionally feeble, and a lamina of the same length as the stipe, or longer. With regard to the muciferous lacunæ by *L. digitata* I have before stated their variation, and also that they most often are wanted by specimens of f. *genuina*, and often also by the other forms from the open coast of Finmarken. I have numerous such specimens. And I have of late had the opportunity of seing that they not always exist by specimens from other places. By the kindness of Geo. W. Traill, Joppa, and J. W. Cursiter, Kirkwall, I have got some almost fresh specimens of *L. digitata* from the Orkney Islands. They are most nearly related to f. *genuina*, and muciferous lacunæ are wanting. On the other hand, by specimens from the southern coast of Norway the lacunæ mostly exist and are as a rule pretty numerous. The same is the case by the specimens, that I have referred to f. *stenophylla*, muciferous lacunæ sometimes exist sometimes are wanting. Therefore, I am still inclined to denie its right to be regarded as a separate species, and keep it as a form of *L. digitata*.

A form of *L. digitata* appears in rock-pools between tides. It is most nearly related partly to f. *genuina*, partly to f. *ensifolia*, and also much varying. The stipe has a height of 1—2 cm. by a lamina 1 m. and more in length, or the stipe becomes about 50 cm. heigh, with shorter lamina, more or less cut up in broader or narrower segments, and the base sometimes cordate, sometimes cuneate. It is annual, at least at Tromsö, arising in April and disappearing in November.

The species in question is litoral and sublitoral, living chiefly in the upper part of the sublitoral zone from extreme low-water mark to a depth of 10—15 fathoms, or probably descending farther down. In the litoral zone I have only seen it in rock-pools between half tide and low-water mark. In much exposed localities f. *genuina* and f. *grandifolia* are vigorous and luxuriant. The former also grows in sheltered places, or even in the interior of deep bays. I do not know when the plant develop its reproductive organs.

Distribution: Common and very abundant especially along the unsheltered part of the coast, but also pretty plentiful in the interior of the deep fjords. The forms *valida*, *complanata* and *stenophylla* only found at Berlevaag; f. *grandifolia* at Berlevaag and Kiberg, but probably more commonly dispersed; f. *ensifolia* scattered and, as far as I know, rather scarce.

Laminaria intermedia Fosl.
Lam. Norw. p. 81.

f. *longipes* Fosl.
l. c. p. 82.
Descr. Laminaria intermedia f. longipes Fosl. l. c.
Fig.   „   „   „   „ t. 7—8

f. *cucullata* (Le Jol.) Fosl.
l. c. p. 82; Laminaria flexicaulis c. cucullata Le Jol. Exam. p. 59.
Descr. Laminaria intermedia f. cucullata Fosl. l. c. p. 88.
        „   flexicaulis c. cucullata Le Jol. l. c.
Fig.   „   intermedia f. cucullata Fosl. l. c. t. 9 et t. 10, fig. 1—16.
Exsicc. „   digitata b. Aresch. Alg. Scand exsicc. No. 167; part. f. cucullata, part. f. ovata.
Syn. Laminaria digitata b. latifolia Aresch. Phyc. Scand. p. 344; excl. syn.
     „   flexicaulis f. latilaciniata Fosl. Bidr. p. 21.
     „   „   subf. latifolia Aresch. Obs. Phyc. 4, p. 10
     „   digitata Kjellm. N. Ish. Algfl. p. 299; ex parte.
     „   cucullata Fosl. Bidr. p. 25.
     „   digitata b. integrifolia J. G. Ag. Lam. p. 24?

This species is most nearly related to *L. digitata*, but,

on the other hand, it sometimes reminds of certain forms of *L. saccharina*. It is an easely recognized species, living in pools at low-water mark, or more commonly in the uppermost part of the sublitoral zone. It thrives best in sheltered places but has also been found in rather exposed localities. It is a proportionally small *Laminaria*, though the lamina often becomes pretty large. The stipe is always feeble and pliable, mostly prostrate, either very short (f. *cucullata*) or elongated (f. *longipes*), though never reaching any considerable length. It is unknown to me when the plant develops its reproductive organs.

Distribution: Found at Sværholt (f. *cucullata*), rare, and at Berlevaag (f. *longipes* and f. *cucullata*), local and scarce.

Fam. Chordaceæ (Kütz.) Rke.
Ostseefl. p. 62; Kütz. Phyc. gen. p. 333; lim. mut.

Gen. Chorda (Stackh.) Lamour.
Ess. p. 46; Stackh. Ner. Brit. p. XVI; ex parte.

Chorda filum (L.) Stackh.
l. c. Fucus filum L. Spec. Pl. p. 1162.

f. *typica*.

Descr. Chorda filum Aresch. Obs. Phyc. 3, p. 13.
Fig. „ „ Harv. Phyc. Brit. t. 107.
Exsicc. „ „ Aresch. Alg. Scand. exsicc. No. 92.

f. *subtomentosa* Aresch.

Obs. Phyc. 3, p. 13.
Descr. Chorda filum β subtomentosa Aresch. l. c.
Exsicc. Chorda filum var. subtomentosa Aresch. Alg. Scand. exsicc. No. 168.
Syn. Fucus filum Gunn. Fl. Norv.
„ „ Wg. Fl. Lapp. p. 505.

This species is in general sublitoral, living chiefly in the uppermost part of the zone on a depth of 1—3 fathoms,

The typical form not seldom occurs in rock-pools between tides, but here it is always feebly developed. The plant appears in the inner part of deep bays as well as on open and exposed coasts, but it thrives best in somewhat sheltered localities, almost ever gregarious. It attains a length of until 3—4 m., but is mostly shorter. Specimens with young zoosporangia have been taken in the beginning of August.

Distribution: Pretty common along the whole coast, entering the inner end of the deeper bays and at some places abundant (f. *typica*); the form *subtomentosa*, according to my experience, is scarce everywhere.

Chorda tomentosa Lyngb.
Hydr. Dan. p. 74.

f. *typica*.
Descr. Chorda tomentosa Aresch. Obs. Phyc. 3, p. 14.
Fig. „ „ Lyngb. l. c. t. 19, fig. A.
Exsicc. „ „ Aresch. Alg. Scand. exsicc. No. 93.

f. *subfulva* nob.
f. minore, debiliore, pilis subfulvis, siccata viridibus; zoosporangiis subellipticis vel oblongo-linearibus.

The form that I have called f. *subfulva* I at first thought to be most nearly related to *Ch. abbreviata*, which A r e s c h o u g in his Obs. Phyb. 3, p. 15 states to have the habit of *Ch. tomentosa*. And the spores and paranemata of the first specimens I found were like those of *Ch. abbreviata*. However, by most of the other specimens, I later collected, the spores and paranemata were in shape almost similar to those of *Ch. tomentosa* f. *typica*. K j e l l m a n has had the kindness to compare it with the original specimen of *Ch. abbreviata* A r e s c h., but this species is said to be more like a young and slender *Ch. filum*. The form *subfulva* is smaller and more slender than the typical form, attaining a length of about 1 m., though mostly only half the length or less. The hairs are more tender and their cells shorter than by f. *ty-*

pica, the colour lighter (between f. *typica* and *Ch. filum*), and they get green after drying. By f. *typica* the hairs keep their colour in drying, or get a little darker. The spores were by some specimens elliptic or subelliptic, 35—48 μ long and 12—16 μ thick, and the paranemata subclavate. By others, and more common, the spores were larger, up to 72 μ long and up to 24 μ thick, and with reference to the shape often agreeing with f. *typica*, though generally thicker in proportion to the length.

The species in question is sublitoral. The typical form lives in similar localities as *Ch. filum*, often growing together with that species. It becomes 2 m. long. At Tromsö it attains a length of about 4 m. The form *subfulva* generally grows in the lower part of the named zone, on a depth of 10—15 fathoms with loose gravelly bottom. I found a solitary specimen on a depth of about 5 fathoms. The species bears zoosporangia in June, and it seems to disappear in the first part of July.

Distribution: The typical form is probably pretty common along the whole coast. I have collected it at Kjöllefjord, local but pretty plentiful, and, according to Areschoug, it has been found at Vardö. The form *subfulva* found at Kjöllefjord, local and rather scarce; and at Mehavn, rare.

Fam. **Asperococcaceæ** Farl.
New. Engl. Alg. p. 88.

Gen. **Asperococcus** Lamour.
Ess. p. 277.

Asperococcus echinatus (Mert.) Grev.

Alg. Brit. p. 50; Conferva echinata Mert. in Roth, Cat. Bot. 3, p. 170.
Descr. Asperococcus echinatus J. G. Ag. Spec. Alg. 1, p. 76.
Fig.   „   „   Harv. Phyc. Brit. t. 194.
Exsicc.   „   „   Aresch, Alg. Scand. exsicc. No. 267,

Litoral, growing in rock-pools in the lower part of the zone. I have only found a solitary and dwarfed specimen, bearing young zoosporangia in the beginning of July.

Distribution: Only found at Berlevaag, a single specimen.

Fam. **Ralfsiaceæ** Farl.
New. Engl. Alg. p. 86.

Gen. **Ralfsia** Berk.
Engl. Bot. Suppl. t. 2866

R a l f s i a d e u s t a (Ag.) J. G. Ag.

Ralfsia (?) deusta J. G. Ag. Spec. Alg. 1. p. 63; Zonaria deusta Ag. Syn. Alg. p. 40.

Descr.. Ralfsia (?) deusta J. G. Ag. l. c.
      „   „   Farl. New. Engl. Alg. p. 87.
Fig. Fucus fungularis Fl. Dan. t. 420.
Ralfsia deusta Rke Ostseefl. p. 48, fig. c.
Syn. Ralfsia deusta Aresch Phyc. Scand. p. 361.

According to A r e s c h o u g, this species has been found at Vardö.

Fam. **Chordariaceæ** (Ag.) Rke.
Ostseefl. p. 39; Ag. Syst. Alg. p. XXXVI; lim. mut.

Gen. **Chordaria** (Ag.) J. G. Ag.
Alg. Syst. 2, p. 62; Ag. Syn. Alg. p. XII; lim. mut.

C h o r d a r i a f l a g e l l i f o r m i s (Müll.) Ag.

l. c. Fucus flagelliformis Müll. Fl. Dan. t. 650.
Descr. Chordaria flagelliformis J. G. Ag. Spec. Alg. 1, p. 66; excl. var.
Fig.   „   „   Harv. Phyc. Brit. t. 111.
        „   „   Kütz. Tab. Phyc. 8, t. 11.
Exsicc. „   „   Aresch. Alg. Scand. exsicc. No. 97.

Syn. Conferva dichotoma Gunn. Fl. Norv. 2, p. 105.
„   elongata   „   „ 2, p. 116.
Fucus flagelliformis Wg. Fl. Lapp. p. 505.

All the specimens that I have examined are referrible to the typical form. However I have seen forms sometimes approaching f. *ramusculifera* Kjellm. and sometimes f. *subsimplex* Kjellm. The last named form has been collected at Loppen in West-Finmarken.

The species is litoral and sublitoral. In the former zone it occurs on rocks and stones, in rock-pools, or fastened to other algæ, chiefly *Fucus serratus* and *Halosaccion ramentaceum*. At some places, for inst. Sværholt and Pasvig, it forms a pretty broad border in the lowermost part of the zone, so as to determine essentially the character of the vegetation. In the sublitoral zone, where it seems to be less common than in the litoral one, it is fastened to other algæ or stones, and descends to a depth of about 10 fathoms. I sometimes have met with stems of *Laminaria hyperborea* and *L. digitata* quite invested with this plant. It appears on open as well as sheltered coasts, but it seems to thrive best in rather exposed places. Specimens bearing zoosporangia have been collected in the later half of June, in July and August.

Distribution: Common and abundant almost everywhere.

Gen. Eudesme J. G. Ag.
Alg. Syst 2, p. 28.

Eudesme virescens (Carm.) J. G. Ag.

l. c. p. 31; Mesogloia virescens Carm. in Hook. Brit. Fl. 2, p. 387.
Descr. Eudesme virescens J. G. Ag. l. c.

Mesogloia virescens J. G. Ag. Spec. Alg. 1, p. 56.
Fig. „   „   Harv. Phyc. Brit. t. 92.
„   „   „   Ner Am. 1, t. 10, fig. b.
Exsicc. Castagnea virescens Aresch. Alg. Scand. exsicc. No. 315.
Syn. Castagnea virescens Kleen, Nordl. Alg. p. 34.
„   Zosteræ Kleen, l. c.; sec. Kjellm. l. c., p. 312.

This species occurs in rock-pools between tides, or in the upper part of the sublitoral zone, on a depth of 2—5 fathoms. It is most often to be met with on open coasts, and here it attains a length of 30 cm., usually 10—15 cm. It bears zoosporangia in the later part of June and, more richly, in July.

Distribution: Scattered along the whole coast, at some places (Berlevaag, Mehavn) common but not plentiful.

Gen. Leathesia (Gray.) J. G. Ag.
Alg. Syst. 2, p. 40; Gray. Brit. Pl. 1, p. 301; char. mut.

Leathesia difformis (L.) Aresch.
Phyc. Scand. p. 376; Tremella difformis L. Fl. Suec. p. 429.
Descr. Leathesia marina J. G. Ag. Spec. Alg. 1, p. 52.
Fig.   "   tuberiformis Harv. Phyc. Brit. t. 324.
    Corynephora baltica Kütz. Tab. Phyc. 8, t. 2.
         "   marina Kütz. l. c. t. 3.
Exsicc. Leathesia difformis Aresch. Alg Scand. exsicc. No. 101 et 214.
    "   "   Hauck et Richt. Phyc. univ. No. 172.
Syn. Chætophora marina Lyngb. Hydr. Dan. p. 193.

A litoral alga, growing in rock-pools in the upper part of the zone, fastened to *Cladophora gracilis*. I have only seen a few dwarfish specimens.

Distribution: Only found at Berlevaag, very rare.

Fam Myrionemaceæ (Thur.)
in Le Jol. Liste Alg. Cherb. p. 15; lim. mut.

Gen. Myrionema Grev.
Crypt. Fl. No. 300, sec. J. G. Ag. Spec. Alg. 1, p. 47.

Myrionema strangulans Grev.
l. c.
Descr. Myrionema strangulans Harv. Phyc. Brit. t. 280,

Fig. Myrionema strangulans Harv. l. c.
" " Kütz. Tab. Phyc. 7, t. 93
" " maculiforme Kütz. l. c.
Exsicc. " " vulgare Aresch. Alg. Scand. exsicc. No. 415.
" " Hauck et Richt. Phyc. univ. No. 169.
Syn. Myrionema vulgare Kleen, Nordl. Alg. p. 35.

Litoral, attached to *Ulvaceæ* and *Cladophora*, bearing zoosporangia in August.

Distribution: Found at Sværholt and Vardö, scarce.

Fam. Lithodermaceæ Hauck,
Meeresalg. p. 402.

Gen. Lithoderma Aresch.
Obs. Phyc. 3, p. 22.

Lithoderma fatiscens Aresch.
l. c. p. 23.
Descr. Lithoderma fatiscens Aresch. l. c.
Fig. " " Hauck, Meeresalg. fig. 177.
" " Kjellm. N. Ish. Algfl. t. 26, fig. 6—7.

The species is sublitoral, growing on stones and *Lithothamnia* on a depth of 3—20 fathoms. Besides typical specimens I at several places also met with a pretty large number of small and barren ones fastened to *Lithothamnia*. They resemble *Lithoderma* but are forming numerous small spots on the host plant. I think they are referrible to the species in question.

Distribution: Found at Kjelmö, Vadsö, Vardö, Mehavn and Lebesby, rather scarce; and at Kjöllefjord, local but pretty plentiful.

Fam. Elachistaceæ Rke
Ostseefl. p. 39.

Gen. **Leptonema** Rke.
Br. Alg. p. 16.

Leptonema fasciculatum Rke.
l. c.

f. *majus* Rke
Ostseefl. p. 51.

Descr. Leptonema fasciculatum var. majus Rke l. c.
Fig. „ „ „ „ Rke Atlas t. 10, fig. 1—9.

A sublitoral alga, occurring on a depth of 10—15 fathoms, attached to *Lithothamnia*. It bears zoosporangia (sparingly) and gametangia in the beginning of August.

Distribution: Only found at Kjelmö in Sydvaranger, local and scarce.

Gen. **Elachista** Duby.
Mem. Cer. I, p. 19, sec. J. G. Ag. Spec. Alg. 1, p. 7.

Elachista fucicola (Vell.) Aresch.
Alg. Pugill. p. 235; Conferva fucicola Vell. Mar. Plant. No. 4, sec. Aresch. l. c.

Descr. Elachista fucicola Aresch. Phyc. Scand p. 377.
„ „ J. G. Ag. Spec. Alg. 1, p. 12.
Fig. „ „ Aresch. l. c. t. 9, fig. c.
„ „ Harv. Phyc. Brit. t. 240.
Phycophila fucorum Kütz. Tab. Phyc. 7, t. 95.

Exsicc. Elachista fucicola Aresch. Alg. Scand. exsicc. No. 102.

Syn. Conferva fucicola Wg. Fl. Lapp. p. 514.
„ flaccida Lyngb. Hydr. Dan. p. 146.

I have met with this species only in the litoral zone, where it occasionally grows on *Fuci*. It bears zoosporangia in June, July and August.

Distribution: Scattered along the whole coast, at several places pretty plentiful.

Elachista lubrica Rupr.
Alg. Och. p. 388.

Descr. Elachista lubrica Aresch. Obs. Phyc. 3, p. 18.
Exsicc.   „   „   „   Alg. Scand. exsicc. No. 217.

This species is litoral and sublitoral. In the former case it occurs gregarious and at many places in great abundance. It is usually fastened to *Halosaccion ramentaceum* and *Rhodomela lycopodioides*, but often also to other species as *Fuci*, *Cystoclonium purpurascens*, *Enteromorpha compressa* and *Desmarestia acuelata*. In the sublitoral zone it has been found scattered on a depth of 5—15 fathoms. It thrives best on open coasts, but enters also nearly to the inner end of the deeper bays. It bears zoosporangia in June, July and August.

Distribution: Common and abundant especially along the open part of the coast.

Fam. Coilodesmeæ nob.

Gen. Coilodesme Strömf.
Meeresalg. Isl. p. 173.

Coilodesme bulligera Strömf.
l. c.

Descr. Coilodesme bulligera Strömf. Algveg. Isl. p. 48.
Fig.   „   „   „   •   t. 2, fig. 9—12.

I found this species already in 1882, or the year before Strömfelt detected it at the coast of Iceland, but as I then only found barren specimens, it was put a side till I again met with it in 1887, bearing zoosporangia.

The Finmarkian specimens seem, with reference to the habit and external appearance, to differ somewhat from the Icelandic ones. Only a few specimens that I collected last year appear to coincide with the latter. The colour is, however, light olive brown. But almost all the specimens formerly taken are gutshaped, more or less inflated and very dark olive brown. The filiform basal part of the thallom is sometimes divided and bears two bandshaped branches.

The plant is litoral, living in pools in the lower part of the zone. It grows somewhat gregarious and occurs only on open coast. The length of the plant is, as at Iceland, generally 10—15 cm., but sometimes reaching about 45 cm. Specimens with zoosporangia have been taken in the middle of July.

Distribution: Found at Kiberg in the neighbourhood of Vardö, in 1882 local but abundant, in 1889 appeared on the same locality only a few small and rather stunted specimens. Also found at Havningberg, very rare, and at Berlevaag, local and scarce.

Fam. Scytosiphoneæ Thur.
in Le Jol. Liste Alg. Cherb. p. 14.

Gen. Phyllitis (Kütz.) Le Jol.
Liste Alg. Cherb. p. 68; Kütz. Phyc. gener. p. 342, lim. mut.

Phyllitis fascia (Müll.) Kütz.
l. c. p. 343; Fucus fascia Müll. Fl. Dan. t. 768.
Descr. Laminaria cæspitosa J. G. Ag. Spec. Alg. 1, p. 130.
    Phyllitis fascia Rke Ostseefl. p. 62.
Fig. Laminaria fascia Harv. Phyc. Brit. t. 45.
    Phyllitis cæspitosa Born. et Thur. Etud. Phycol. t. 4.
    Phycolapathum cuneatum Kütz. Tab. Phyc. 6, t. 49.
Exsicc. Laminaria fascia Aresch. Alg. Scand. exsicc. Ed. 1, No. 36.
    „   „   Wyatt, Alg. Danm. No. 157.
    Phyllitis cæspitosa Le Jol. Alg. mar. Cherb. No. 154.
    Ilea fascia Aresch. Alg. Scand exsicc. No. 96; spec. thall. latiore.
Syn. Ulva fascia Lyngb. Hydr. Dan. t. 119.
    Ilea fascia Aresch. Phyc. Scand. p. 353; ex parte.
    „   „   Kjellm. N. Ish. Algfl. p. 319; ex parte fide syn.

This species is rather a pelagic plant, common and luxuriant developed on open coasts, or else in exposed localities, but growing in sheltered places, or entering into deep bays, it becomes more and more narrow. At Finmarken as well as farther south I along open coast only have met with but the broad form (*Ph. cæspitosa*), and, on the other hand, only the narrow one in the inner part of deep bays. Here the latter is most often 1.5—4 mm. broad and generally more or less twisted, but sometimes growing even in these places gregarious in a large number of individuals.

The species is litoral, chiefly occurring in pools between tides, usually fastened to smaller stones, more seldom to rocks and exceptionally to other algæ, as *Halosaccion ramentaceum* and *Fuci*. It is smaller at East- than at West-Finmarken, generally about 10 cm. long, seldom attaining a length of 25—30 cm. It bears reproductive organs in August, in Tromsö amt in the later half of July.

Distribution: Common and pretty plentiful almost everywhere.

Gen. **Scytosiphon** (Ag.) Thur.
in Le Jol. Liste Alg. Cherb. p. 20; Ag. Spec. Alg. 1, p. 160; char. mut

Scytosiphon lomentarius (Lyngb.) J. G. Ag.
Spec. Alg. 1, p. 126; Chorda lomentaria Lyngb. Hydr. Dan. p. 74.

f. *typica*.

Descr. Scytosiphon lomentarius J. G. Ag. l. c.
Fig. Chorda lomentaria Harv. Phyc. Brit. t. 285.
Scytosiphon lomentarius Aresch. Obs. Phyc. 3, t. 2, fig. 1.
Exsicc. Chorda lomentaria Aresch. Älg. Scand. exsicc. No. 94.

f. *fistulosa* (Ag.)
Chorda filum β fistulosa Ag. Syn. p. 14.
Descr. Chorda filum ♂ fistulosa Kütz. Spec. Alg. p. 548.
Fig.   „   „   „   „   Tab. Phyc. 8, t. 14 et 15, fig. d—e.
Exsicc. „ lomentaria var. autumnalis Aresch. Alg. Scand. exsicc. No. 95.
  „   „   b. Aresch. l. c. No. 169.

Syn. Chorda lomentaria Aresch. Phyc. Scand. p. 365.
Fucus lomentarius Sommerf. Suppl. p. 184.[1])

The form *fistulosa* seems to me to be a pretty well marked one. It is smaller than the typical form, and distinguishes itself, besides not being constricted, by the form of the paraphyses. These are most often rather numerous and generally clavate or subclavate, with a much attenuated base. The hairs are few or often wanting.

The species in question is litoral, chiefly occurring at low-water mark, and here it often grows gregarious in a great number of individuals. It thrives best on open coasts, is here vigorously developed, attaining a length of 1 m. and more, but occurs also in sheltered places. The form *fistulosa* lives in the same localities as f. *typica*, though occosionally in rockpools and higher up than the latter. Specimens bearing gametangia have been collected in the later half of June, in July and in the beginning of August.

Distribution: Common along the whole coast and at several places abundant, as Kjöllefjord, Mehavn, Finkongkjeilen, Syltefjord.

Gen. **Physematoplea** Kjellm. mscr.

P h y s e m a t o p l e a a t t e n u a t a Kjellm.
N. Ish. Algfl. p. 321.
Descr. Scytosiphon attenuatus Kjellm. l. c.
Fig.   „   „   „   „   t. 26, fig. 1—5.

This alga is litoral, growing in rock-pools on exposed places. It is here smaller and thinner than at the coasts of Spitzbergen, 3—7 cm. long. It bears zoosporangia in the middle of July. At West-Finmarken it has been taken with

---

[1]. It has been shown that *Chordaria attenuata* F o s l. in Tromsö Mus. Aarsh. X. p. 176 is a *Scytosiphon*, but I do not know, yet, whether referrible to *S. lomentarius*.

zoosporangia and gametangia at the end of May. The zoosporangia are situated as the gametangia, on different individuals, mostly obovate, 42—60 µ long and 28—36 µ broad.

Distribution: Only found at Bugönæs in Sydvaranger, very rare.

Fam. **Punctariaceæ** (Thur.) Kjellm.
Pl. Scand. p. 9; Thur. in Le Jol. Liste Alg. Cherb. p. 14; lim. mut.

Gen. **Desmotrichum** Kütz.
Phyc. germ. p. 244.

Desmotrichum undulatum (J. G. Ag.) Rke.
Ostseefl. p. 55; Punctaria undulata J. G. Ag. Nov. p. 15, sec. Spec. Alg. 1, p. 72.
Descr. Desmotrichum undulatum Rke l. c. p. 57.
    Punctaria undulata J. G. Ag. Spec. Alg. 1, p. 72.
Fig. Desmotrichum undulatum Rke. Atlas t. 11.
    „   tenuissimum Kütz. Tab. Phyc. 6, t. 44.
Exsicc. Punctaria undulata Aresch. Alg. Scand. exsicc. No. 90.
    Syn. Ulva plantaginifolia Lyngb. Hydr. Dan. p. 31.

I found, in the middle of June, some young and barren specimens of an alga, which I think are to be referred to this species. They grew in a rock-pool in the lower part of the litoral zone, fastened to *Ceramium rubrum*, in a somewhat exposed locality.

Distribution: Only found at Kjöllefjord, very rare.

Gen. **Punctaria** Grev.
Alg. Brit. p. XLII.

Punctaria plantaginea (Roth) Grev.
l. c. p. 53; Ulva plantaginea Roth, Cat. Bot. 2, p. 243.
f. *typica*.

Descr. Punctaria plantaginea J. G. Ag. Spec. Alg. 1, p. 73.
Fig.   „   „   Harv. Phyc. Brit. t. 128.
      Phycolapathum plantagineum Kütz. Tab. Phyc. 6, t. 48.
           „   fissum Kütz. l. c.
Exsicc. Punctaria plantaginea Aresch. Alg. Scand. exsicc. No. 170.
          „   „   Hauck et Richt. Phyc. univ. No. 166.

f. *linearis* Fosl.
   Arct. havalg. p. 9.
Descr. Punctaria plantaginea β linearis Fosl. l. c.
   Syn. Ulva rubescens Lyngb. Hydr. Dan. p. 27.
         „   „   Sommerf. in Act. Nidros p. 51.
       Fucus   „   „   Suppl. p. 183.

Litoral, occurring in rock-pools in the lower part of the region, on open as well as sheltered coasts, but not in much exposed localities. It bears zoosporangia in the later half of July and the first part of August. A transition between f. *typica* and f. *linearis* has been taken at Bugönæs and Vadsö.

Distribution: Scattered and very scarce along the whole coast.

Fam. Desmarestiaceæ Thur.
in Le Jol. Liste Alg. Cherb. p. 14.

Gen. Desmarestia (Lamour.) Grev.
Alg. Brit. p. XXXIX; Lamour. Ess. p. 43; spec. excl.

Desmarestia acuelata (L.) Lamour.
   l. c. p. 45; Fucus acuelatus L. Spec. Pl. Ed. 2, p. 1632.
Descr. Desmarestia acuelata J. G. Ag. Spec. Alg. 1, p. 167.
Fig.   „   „   Harv. Phyc. Brit. t. 49.
           „   „   Kütz. Tab. Phyc. 9, t. 94.
           „   hybrida   „   „   9, t. 93.
Exsicc.   „   acuelata Aresch. Alg. Scand. exsicc. No. 87 et 165.
   Syn. Desmia acuelata Lyngb. Hydr. Dan. p. 34.
      Fucus acuelatus β Wg. Fl. Lapp. p. 502.
     „   virgatus Gunn. Fl. Norv. 1, p. 45.

Syn. Fucus muscoides Gunn. l. c. 2, p. 139.

This species is, in general, sublitoral, but it occurs sometimes also in the litoral zone, in rock-pools, where I have seen solitary specimens fastened to *Fuci*. It is most frequent and best developed on a depth of 2—10 fathoms, chiefly on open coast, and often gregarious in pretty large masses.

Distribution: Common along the whole coast and at many places abundant.

Gen. Dichloria Grev.
Alg. Brit. p. XL.

Dichloria viridis (Müll.) Grev.
l. c p. 39; Fucus viridis Müll. Fl. Dan. t. 886.
Descr. Dichloria J. G. Ag. Spec. Alg. 1, p. 164.
Fig. Desmarestia viridis Harv. Phyc. Brit. p. 312.
    „   „ Kütz. Tab. Phyc. 9, t. 92.
Exsicc. „   „ Aresch. Alg. Scand. exsicc. No. 88.
   Syn. Fucus viridis Wg. Fl. Lapp. p. 503.
     Gigartina viridis Lyngb. Hydr. Dan. p. 44.

This plant is sublitoral, and it thrives best on open coast, usually on a depth of 2—10 fathoms and a bottom formed of pebbles, shells and *Lithothamnia*, descending to 15 fathoms or perhaps farther down. It is in general fastened to smaller stones or to *Lithothamnia*, growing gregarious and often in considerable masses. In a place in the neighbourhood of Tromsö the plant is partly also litoral, forming a broad belt from about 2 feet below to a little above extreme low-water mark, and, consequently, uncovered at lowest spring tides. Here it arises in May and disappears in October. I do not know when it develops its reproductive organs.

Distribution: Common along the whole coast and at many places abundant.

Fam. Dictyosiphoneæ Thur.
in Le Jol. Liste Alg. Cherb. p. 14.

Gen. Phloeospora Aresch.[1]
Bot. Not. 1873, p. 163.

Phloeospora subarticulata Aresch.
l. c. p. 164.
Descr. Phloeospora subarticulata Aresch. Bot. Not. 1876, p. 33.
Fig. Dictyosiphon foeniculaceus β b. Aresch. Phyc. Scand. t. 5, fig. F.
      "   "   Lyngb. Hydr. Dan. t. 14 C. fig. 3.
Phloeospora subarticulata Aresch. Obs. Phyc. 3, t. 3, fig. 2—5.
Exsicc. Dictyosiphon foeniculaceus var. subarticulatus Aresch. Alg. Scand.
exsicc. No. 104 et 318.

This is, as far as I have seen, an alga sparingly dispersed along the coast of East-Finmarken. I have found it only at two places, growing in rock-pools in the lower part of the litoral zone, and in the sublitoral zone on a depth of 4—6 fathoms.

Distribution: Only found at Berlevaag and Vadsö, very rare.

Phloeospora tortilis (Rupr.) Aresch.
Bot. Not. 1876, p. 34; Scytosiphon tortilis Rupr. Alg. Och. p. 373.
Descr. Phloeospora tortilis Aresch. l. c.
Fig. Dictyosiphon tortilis Gobi, Brauntange t. 2, fig. 12—16.
Phloeospora tortilis Kjellm. Spetsb. Thall. 2, t. 1, fig. 1.
Exsicc.   "   "   Aresch. Alg. Scand. exsicc. No. 413.

Litoral (and sublitoral?), appearing on open coast as well as in the interior of the fjords. Zoospore-bearing specimens have been collected at the end of August, at West-Finmarken in the middle of the named month.

Distribution: Commonly diffused along the whole coast, at some places, for inst Berlevaag and Kirkenæs, abundant but local.

---

[1]. I keep this genus distinct from *Stictyosiphon* Kütz. following Kjellman's apprehension.

Gen. Gobia Rke.
Ostseefl. p. 65.

Gobia baltica (Gobi) Rke.
l. c. Cladosiphon balticus Gobi, Brauntange p. 12.

Descr. Gobia baltica Rke l. c.

Fig. Cladosiphon balticus Gobi, l. c. t. 1, fig. 7—11.
Gobia baltica Rke l. c. fig. 3.

Exsicc. Coilonema Chordaria var. simpliciuscula Aresch. Alg. Scand exsicc.
No. 323.
Dictyosiphon (Coilonema) Chordaria f. simplex Aresch. l. c. No. 412.

Syn. Dictyosiphon (Coilonema) Chordaria b. simpliciuscula Aresch.
Bot. Not. 1873, p. 170 et Obs. Phyc. 3, p. 32.

A few unbranched specimens of this alga I collected in Varangerfjord, in rock-pools in the lower part of the litoral zone, bearing zoosporangia in the middle of July.

Distribution: Found at Bugönæs in Sydvaranger, rare.

Gen. Coilonema Aresch.
Alg. Scand. exsicc. No. 323.

Coilonema Ekmani Aresch.
Obs. Phyc. 3, p. 33.

Descr. Dictyosiphon (Coilonema) Ekmani Aresch. l. c.

Syn. Lithosiphon Laminariæ Kleen, Nordl. Alg. p. 40, sec. Kjellm.
N. Ish. Algfl. p. 329.

This species grows epiphytic on *Scytosiphon lomentarius* in the lowermost part of the litoral zone, on open coast. It is smaller than farther south, 1—3 cm. long. Specimens collected in the middle of July were provided with young zoosporangia.

Distribution: Found at Kjöllefjord and Særholt, scarce.

Coilonema chordaria Aresch.
Bot. Not. 1873, p. 170.

f. *bahusiensis* Aresch.
l. c.

Descr. Dictyosiphon (Coilonema) chordaria Áresch. Obs. Phyc. 3, p. 32.
Fig. „ chordaria Aresch. Phyc. Scand. t. 8, B.
Syn. Dictyosiphon (Coilonema) Finmarkicum Fosl. Arct. havalg. p. 6·

A litoral plant, in general occurring in rock-pools in the upper part of the zone, on open coast. Large and well developed specimens have been collected at Vardö, attaining a length of 25 cm. It bears zoosporangia in August. The plant described by me some years ago (l. c.) under the name of *Dictyosiphon (Coilonema) Finmarkicum* is identic with the above quoted form of the present species.

Distribution: Found at Sværholt, local and rather scarce, Vardö, local but abundant, and at Bugönæs, rare.

Coilonema filiformis Fosl.
in Tromsö Mus. Aarsh. 10, p. 178.
Descr. Coilonema filiformis Fosl. l. c.
Fig. „ „ „ „ t. 3, fig. 1—2.

This species seems to be well differentiated. However the specimens at my disposal are rather few and badly preserved, found among earlier collections from Finmarken. The plant is litoral, growing in rock-pools in somewhat exposed localities. I have only a couple of barren specimens from East-Finmarken, but at West-Finmarken it has been taken with zoosporangia at the end of June.

Distribution: Only found at Berlevaag, very rare.

Gen. Dictyosiphon (Grev.) Aresch.
Bot. Not. 1873, p. 164; Grev. Alg. Brit. p. 55; char. mut.

Dictyosiphon corymbosus Kjellm.
N. Ish. Algfl. p. 330.
Descr. Dictyosiphon corymbosus Kjellm. l. c.
Fig. „ „ „ „ t. 26, fig. 12—15. (f. abbreviata).

I met with some few specimens of a *Dictyosiphon*, which I think are to be referred to this species and seem to be most nearly related to f. *abbreviata*. They are more tenuous than specimens of that form from Novaya Zemlya, and, as they are sterile, the determination is not quite sure. However, with reference to the ramification they coincide well with the present species.

Distribution: Found at Kjöllefjord, rare.

Dictyosiphon fragilis Harv.
in Kütz. Spec. Alg. p. 485.
Descr. Dictyosiphon fragilis Kütz. l. c.
Fig. „ „ „ Tab. Phyc. 6, t. 52.
Syn. Dictyosiphon hippuroides f. fragilis Kjellm. N. Ish. Algfl. p. 332.

It seems to me that among the numerous forms of *D. hippuroides* also occurring along the northern coast of Norway, *D. fragilis* is one of the more distinctly marked ones, and, by a severance of *D. hippuroides*, ought to be regarded as a distinct species of the same degree as *D. corymbosus*. I at least found it pretty well differentiated, but, according to Kjellman, it shall not always be independant, approaching so nearly to *D. hippuroides* that it is difficult to draw a limit between them. However, the same is the case with *D. corymbosus* too, as far as I am able to judge, and even between *D. hippuroides* and *D. foeniculaceus* is the limit often difficult to draw.

The species is characterized by its loose consistency, mostly distinct main axis and coarse, often more or less flexuous branches increasing in thickness upwards. The colour is darker than by *D. hippuroides*, sometimes inclining to rusty brown. Dried specimens are more difficult to distinguish from the latter because it dwindles much in drying, owing to its loose consistency, and looks equal in thickness, but, on the other hand, it becomes still darker and sometimes assumes an almost black colour. The zoosporangia are generally larger than by the last named species, and more numerous.

The present plant is litoral, living in rock-pools in the upper part of the zone, and appears only on open coasts. It bears zoosporangia in the middle of July.

Distribution: Found at Mehavn, scarce, at Berlevaag, local but abundant, and at Ekkerö, scarce.

Dictyosiphon hippuroides (Lyngb.) Kütz.

Tab. Phyc. 6, p. 19; Scytosiphon hippuroides Lyngb. Hydr. Dan. p. 63.
Descr. Dictyosiphon hippuroides Aresch. Obs. Phyc. 3, p. 26.
Fig. „ „ Kütz. l. c. t. 52.
Exsicc. „ „ Aresch. Alg. Scand. exsicc. No. 105, 320, 321.

Syn. Dictyosiphon foeniculaceus α Aresch. Phyc. Scand. p. 147.

This species is chiefly litoral, usually living in rock-pools fastened to stones, or, more often, epiphytic on other algæ, principally *Chordaria flagelliformis* and *Fuci*, sometimes also *Rhodymenia palmata* and *Halosaccion ramentaceum*. It occurs on open as well as sheltered coasts. Specimens bearing zoosporangia have been taken in June, July and August.

Distribution: Common and abundant almost everywhere.

Dictyosiphon foeniculaceus (Huds.) Grev.

Alg. Brit. p. 56; Conferva foeniculacea Huds. Fl. Angl. p. 164.

f. *typica*.

Descr. Dictyosiphon foeniculaceus Aresch. Obs. Phyc. 3, p. 30.
Fig. „ „ „ Phyc. Scand. t. 7.
Exsicc. „ „ „ Alg. Scand. exsicc. No. 103, 319.

f. *flaccida* Aresch.

Bot. Not. 1873, p. 137
Descr. Dictyosiphon foeniculaceus var. flaccidus Aresch. Obs. Phyc. 3, p. 31.

Syn. Scytosiphon foenisulaceus Lyngb. Hydr. Dan. p. 63; ex parte.
Dictyosiphon foeniculaceus β Aresch. Phyc. Scand. p. 148.

The form *flaccida* is, in the Norwegian Polar Sea, a well differentiated form. Its zoosporangia are generally larger than by the typical form, their long axis attains sometimes even 110 μ. At Tromsö occurs a very coarse form, most nearly related to f. *flaccida*, but it ought perhaps to be kept distinct. I think to have seen it also at Finmarken.

The species in question is litoral, growing in tidal pools epiphytic on other algæ, usually *Fuci*, sometimes also *Chordaria flagelliformis*, or fastened to stones. The plant occurs on open coast as well as in the inner of deep bays and seems to prefer somewhat sheltered localities. It bears zoosporangia in June (f. *flaccida*), and in July and August (f. *typica*).

Distribution: Common and plentiful almost everywhere.

Dictyosiphon hispidus Kjellm.
Algenveg. Murm. Meer. p. 47.
Deser. Dictyosiphon foeniculaceus subspec. hispidus Kjellm. Spetsb. Thall. 2, p. 39.
Fig. „ „ „ „ l. c. t. 2, fig. 1.

In the eastern part of the district I collected a few specimens of a *Dictyosiphon*, which I have referred to this species. They do not fully coincide with specimens from Novaya Zemlya, but no doubt they are referrible to the present species. The short secondary branches are less numerous than by the named specimens, and the plant much reminds of *D. foeniculaceus* f. *flaccida*. The plant grews in the litoral zone attached to *Scytosiphon lomentarius*, bearing zoosporangia in the beginning of August, but sparingly.

Distribution: Found only at Vardö, rare.

Fam. **Sphacelariaceæ** J. G. Ag.
Alg. Med. p. 27.

Gen. **Chætopteris** Kütz.
Phyc. gener. p. 293.

Chætopteris plumosa (Lyngb.) Kütz.
l. c. Sphacelaria plumosa Lyngb. Hydr. Dan. p. 103,

Descr. Chætopteris plumosa J. G. Ag. Spec. Alg. 1. p. 41.
Fig.   „   „   Kütz. Tab. Phyc. 6, t. 6.
             „   „   Aresch. Obs. Phyc. 3, t. 2, fig. 4.
             „   „   Kjellm. Spetsb. Thall. 2, t. 2, fig. 2—3,
Exsicc. Sphacelaria plumosa Aresch. Alg. Scand. exsicc. No. 107.
      Chætopteris plumosa Aresch. l. c. No. 408.
   Syn. Conferva pennata Wg. Fl. Lapp p. 512; ex parte.

Litoral and sublitoral. In the former instance growing in rock-pools or on stones at low-water mark. In the latter instance mostly fastened to roots of *Laminaria*, descending to a depth of 10—15 fathoms, on open coasts as well as sheltered ones. It is smaller than farther south, generally 2—4 cm. high. In the summer I have met with but barren specimens. At Nordland it has been found with zoosporangia in March.

In Krit. fortegn. p. 121 I have referred *Fucus hirsutus* Gunn. Fl. Norv. 2, p. 25 to *Cladostephus spongiosus*, according to Gunnerus occurring «in mari finm. rarior». I do not think this species is to be found at the coast of the present Finmarken. It may perhaps have been *Chætopteris plumosa*, or, if *Cladostephus spongiosus*, collected in the most northern part of the present Tromsö amt.

Distribution: Scattered and scarce along the whole coast. Perhaps more commonly diffused within the sublitoral zone than hitherto known.

Gen. **Sphacelaria** (Lyngb.) J. G. Ag.
Spec. Alg. 1, p. 29; Lyngb. Hydr. Dan. p. 103; spec. e cl.

Sphacelaria racemosa Grev.
Scot. Crypt. Fl. 2, t. 96, sec. Harv. Phyc. Brit. t. 349.

f. *arctica* (Harv.) Rke.
Ostseefl. p. 40; Sphacelaria arctica Harv. sec. J. G. Ag. Grönl. Alg. p. 110.

Descr. Sphacelaria arctica Kjellm. Spetsb. Thall. 2, p. 34.

Descr. Sphacelaria racemosa var. arctica Rke l. c
Fig. „ arctica Kjellm. l. c. t. 2, fig. 4—6.
Syn. Conferva pennata Wg. Fl. Lapp. p. 512; ex parte.

According to Reinke l. c., it seems almost to be a fact that *Sphacelaria arctica* is identic with or so nearly related to *Sphacelaria racemosa* that it at most may be regarded as a form of the latter.

The plant is litoral, occurring on rocks or in rock-pools in the lower part of the zone, seldom epiphytic on other algæ, as *Rhodomela lycopodioides*. Probably it also descends into the sublitoral zone. In June, July and August only barren specimens have been found.

Distribntion: Scattered and rather scarce along the whole coast.

Sphacelaria olivacea (Dillw.) Ag.
Spec. Alg. 2, p. 30; Conferva olivacea Dillw. Brit Conf. p. 57.!
Descr. Sphacelaria olivacea J. G. Ag. Spec. Alg. 1, p. 30.
Fig. „ „ Pringsh. Sphac. t. 9, fig. 1—3.
„ „ Traill et Holmes Sphac. t. 2, fig. 2.
Exsicc. „ „ Aresch. Alg. Scand. exsicc. No. 410.

Litoral, growing gregarious mostly on steep rocks and often together with other algæ, as *Rhodochorton Rothii*, *Callithamnion scopulorum*, *Ptilota elegans* and *Delesseria alata*. It occurs on open as well as sheltered coasts. Specimens collected in July and August were sterile.

Distribution: Rather scarce along the whole coast.

Fam. **Ectocarpaceæ** (Ag.) Thur.
in Le Jol. Liste Alg. Cherb. p. 14; Ag. Syst. Alg. p. XXX, lim. mut.

Gen. **Isthmoplea** Kjellm.
Algenv. Murm. Meer. p. 30.

Isthmoplea sphærophora (Harv.) Kjellm.

l. c. Ectocarpus sphærophorus Harv. Engl. Fl. 5, p. 326.
Descr. Capsicarpella sphærophora Kjellm. Scand. Ect. och. Tilopt. p. 20.
Fig. „   „   „   „   „   „   „   t. 1, fig. 2.
Ectocarpus sphærophorus Harv. Phyc. Brit. t. 126.
Exsicc. Capsicarpella sphærophora Aresch. Alg. Scand. exsicc. No. 414.

Litoral and epiphytic on other algæ, as *Rhodomela lycopodioides, Polysiphonia fastigiata, Cystoclonium purpurascens Ptilota pectinata, Ptilota elegans* and *Cladophora rupestris*. It sometimes appears in larger numbers and almost covers the host plant, for inst. *Rh. lycopodioides* at Kjöllefjord. It prefers open coast and does not enter far into the great fjords, and is, in general, smaller than farther south. I have taken it bearing reproductive organs in the later half of June, in July, and in the first part of August.

Distribution: Pretty common along the open part of the coast and at some places abundant.

Gen. Ectocarpus (Lyngb.) Kjellm.

Skand. Ect. och Tilopt. p. 34; Lyngb. Hydr. Dan. p. 130; char. mut.

Ectocarpus confervoides (Roth.) Le Jol.
Liste Alg. Cherb. p. 75, Ceramium confervoides Roth. Cat. Bot. 1, p 151.

f. *arcta* Kütz. (Kjellm.)
l. c. p. 70. Ectocarpus arctus Kütz. Phyc. gener. p. 289.
Descr Ectocarpus confervoides f. arcta Kjellm. l. c. p. 71.
Fig. Corticularia arcta Kütz. Tab. Phyc. 5. t. 80.
Exsicc. Ectocarpus pseudosiliculosus Crouan, Exsicc. No. 27; sec. Kjellm.
N. Ish. Algfl. p. 342.

f. *siliculosa* Dillw. (Kjellm.)
l. c. p. 73; Conferva siliculosa Dillw. Conf. p. 69.
Descr. Ectocarpus confervoides f. siliculosa Kjellm. l. c.
Fig,   „   siliculosus Lyngb. Hydr. Dan. t. 43, fig. e.
Exsicc. „   „   Aresch. Alg. Scand. exsicc. No. 176.

f. *typica* Kjellm.
N. Ish. Algfl. p. 342.

Descr. Ectocarpus confervoides s. s. Kjellm. Scand. Ect. och Tilopt. p. 77.
Fig. „ patens Kütz. Tab. Phyc. 5, t. 67.
Exsicc. „ litoralis var. Aresch. Alg. Scand. exsicc. Nr. 111.

f. *penicillata* Ag.
Spec. Alg. p. 162.
Descr. Ectocarpus confervoides f. penicillata Kjellm. l. c. p. 80.
Fig. Corticularia Nægeliana Kütz. Tab. Phyc. 5, t. 81.
Exsicc. Ectocarpus siliculosus Aresch. Alg. Scand. exsicc. No. 112.
Syn. Conferva litoralis Wg. Fl. Lapp. p. 513; ex parte.
„ (Ectocarpus) siliculosa Sommerf. Suppl. p. 193.

Litoral and sublitoral. In the former zone it occurs chiefly at low-water mark and usually fastened to other algæ, as *Fuci, Chordaria flagelliformis* and *Cladophoræ*. In the sublitoral zone it descends to a depth of about 10 fathoms, generally attached to other algæ, as *Chorda filum* and *Lithothamnia*. It appears on open as well as sheltered coasts, and also enters the inner end of the deep bays. The plant bears gametangia in June, July and August. In the middle of June I found a solitary specimen provided with zoosporangia together with gametangia (f. *siliculosa*).

Distribution: Pretty common everywhere and at several places abundant.

Ectocarpus fasciculatus Harv.
Man. p. 40; ex parte, sec. Kjellm. Scand. Ect. och Tilopt. p. 89.
Descr. Ectocarpus fasciculatus Kjellm. l. c.
Fig. „ „ Harv. Phyc. Brit. t. 273.
Exsicc. „ „ Aresch. Alg. Scand. exsicc. Nr. 114.

Litoral and sublitoral, chiefly fastened to other algæ, as *Cladophora*, the lamina of *Laminaria hyperborea, L. digitata* and the stipe of *Alaria*. It is only met with on open coast, and it bears gametangia in the later half of June, in July and August.

Distribution: Scattered and rather scarce along the unsheltered part of the coast, at some places, for inst. Kjöllefjord, pretty plentiful.

Ectocarpus terminalis Kütz.
Phyc. gener. p. 236.
Descr. Ectocarpus terminalis Kjellm. Skand. Ect. och. Tilopt. p. 54.
Fig.   „   „   „   „   „   t. fig. 7.

A litoral alga, growing epiphytic on *Monostroma* and *Porphyra*. It bears gametangia in the beginning of August.

Distribution: Found only at Vardö, scarce, but probably also occurring in other places.

Ectocarpus repens Rke.
Ostseefl. p. 42.
Descr. Ectocarpus reptans Kjellm. Skand Ect. och. Tilopt. p. 52.
Fig.   „   „   Kjellm. l. c. t. 2, fig. 8.
          „   repens Rke. Atlas t. 19.

Litoral, epiphytic on *Monostroma* together with the preceding species.

Distribution: Found at Vardö, rare.

Gen. Pylaiella Bory.
Dict. Class. 4, p. 393.

Pylaiella (?) curta Fosl.
in Tromsö Mus. Aarsh. 10, p. 181.
Descr. Pylaiella (?) curta Fosl. l. c.
Fig.   „   „   „   „   t. 3, fig. 4—5.

As mentioned in the above quoted paper, it is doubtful whether this species is referrible to the genus *Pylaiella*. It seems rather to form a new genus. But hitherto has only been found one kind of reproductive organs, which is supposed to be gametangia (zoosporangia multilocularia). Unfortunately, the first alcohol material I brought home was not good, and last year I found only a few small and younger specimens.

The plant is litoral. At the only place of growth hitherto known it was fastened to the upper part of the lamina of *Laminaria digitata*, on a somewhat exposed locality, together with *Isthmoplea sphærophora*, *Ectocarpus confervoides* and *Pylaiella litoralis*. It has been taken with reproductive organs at the end of May, and in the middle of June and July.

Distribution: Found only at Mehavn. At the end of May, 1882, and in the middle of June, 1887, local but abundant. In the middle of July, 1889, very rare.

Pylaiella litoralis (L.) Kjellm.

Skand. Ect. och Tilopt. p. 99; Conferva litoralis L. Spec. Plant. p. 1165; ex parte.

Descr. Pylaiella litoralis Kjellm. l. c.

Fig. Ectocarpus litoralis Harv. Phyc. Brit. t. 197.

    „   „ Kütz. Tab. Phyc. 5, t. 76.

    „ compactus Kütz. l. c.

Spongonema castaneum Kütz. l. c.. . 83.

Exsicc. Ectocarpus firmus Aresch. Alg. Scand. exsicc. Nr. 24.

    „   „ var. rupincola Aresch. l. c. Nr. 113.

    „   „ f. vernalis Aresch. l. c. Nr. 173.

Syn. Conferva litoralis Wg. Fl. Lapp. p. 513; ex parte.

This plant does not appear in as many forms as farther south, though also here much varying. It is litoral, sometimes descending into the sublitoral zone, but only in inferior depths. It is mostly fastened to other algæ, as *Fucaceæ*, but also to rocks or stones and woodwork. I have even seen it attached to crabs and fishes *(Cyclopterus)*. It bears zoosporangia in June, July and August, and gametangia in June and July. At Nordland I have taken zoospore-bearing specimens in the middle of December.

Distribution: Common and abundant everywhere.

Pylaiella macrocarpa Fosl.

in Tromsö Mus. Aarsh. 10, p. 179

Descr. Pylaiella macrocarpa Fosl. l. c.

Fig.   „   „   „   „ t. 2, fig. 13—15.

This species is nearly related to certain forms of *Pylaiella litoralis*. It differs by its long chains of zoosporangia and very long gametangia, the former in a number of until 40, the latter 180—1320 µ long, and by the subsecund branches of the last and the last but one order, the latter mostly issuing in pairs.

The plant is litoral and sublitoral. In the former case growing in rock-pools fastened to *Laminaria digitata*. In the latter case attached to the stipe of *Alaria* on a depth of 2—5 fathoms. It bears zoosporangia in June. At Tromsö I have collected specimens with zoosporangia and gametangia in the beginning of August. They have sometimes been found in one and the same individual, or even joining each other.

Distribution: Found at Kjöllefjord, scarce, and at Mehavn, rare.

Pylaiella varia Kjellm.
N. Ish. Algfl. p. 348.
Descr. Pylaiella varia Kjellm. l. c.
Fig. „   „   „   „ t. 27, fig. 1—12.

Sublitoral, occurring on a depth of 2—5 fathoms. Specimens taken in the middle of June were sterile. I have collected zoospore-bearing ones at Tromsö in the beginning of September, in rock-pools between tides among other algæ.

Distribution: Found only at Kjöllefjord, rare.

Ser. Chlorophyceæ (Rabenh.) Wittr.
Pithoph. p. 42; Rabenh. Fl. Eur. Alg. 3, p. 1; lim. mut.

Fam. Ulvaceæ (Ag.) Rke.
Ostseefl. p. IX; Ag. Syst. Alg. p. XXX; lim. mut.

Gen. Monostroma (Thur.) Wittr.
Monostr. p. 15; Thur. Note s. Ulv. p. 29, sec. Wittr. l. c.; lim. mut.

Monostroma latissimum (Kütz.) Wittr.

Monostr. p. 33; Ulva latissima Kütz. Phyc. gener. p. 296.

Descr. Monostroma latissimum Wittr. l. c.
Fig. „ „ „ „ t. 1, fig. 4.
Exsicc. „ „ Wittr. et Nordst. Alg. exsicc. Nr. 145.

Of this species I have only met with a solitary specimen, picked up by the dredge from a depth of about 10 fathoms, and probably having lain loose on the bottom. It is 8 cm. long and 6 cm. broad.

Distribution: Found at Kjöllefjord, a single specimen.

Monostroma undulatum Wittr.

Monostr. p. 46.

f. *typica* nob.

Descr. Monostroma undulatum Wittr. l. c.
Fig. „ „ „ „ t. 3, fig. 9.

f. *Farlowii* nob.

Descr. Monostroma pulchrum Farl. New. Engl. Alg. p. 41.

Syn. Ulva lactuca Wg. Fl. Lapp. p. 507.

I have seen a pretty large number of a *Monostroma* belonging to the same section as *M. latissimum* with the frond membraneously expanding even in a young state. It corresponds well with Wittrock's description of *M. undulatum* except with regard to the structure in the monostromatic part of the frond. But as other species of the genus are rather much varying also in reference to the structure, for inst. *M. arcticum* and *M. saccodeum*, I think it may be referred to the present species. I regard it the typical form. I also met with a few specimens of another *Monostroma* which coincide well with *M. pulchrum* Farl., but, on the other side, so nearly related to *M. undulatum* that no limit hardly can be drawn between them, and, therefore, I keep it a form of the latter, and propose to call it f. *Farlowii*.

The typical form is ovale, ovate-lanceolate, or lanceolate, mostly broadest in the lower part of the frond and from there often attenuated towards the summit. A solitary specimen in my collections is almost reniform and somewhat oblique, 6 cm. long and 10 cm. broad in the broadest part. The largest specimen I have seen is 24 cm. long and 6 cm. broad. In general the plant is smaller, 8 -12 cm. long and 3—6 cm. broad. It is densely folded, the folds extend mostly to the middle line of the frond, and the margin is much crisped. The colour varies between light and rather dark green. The plant has a somewhat loose consistency, is slimy and feebly shining. A cross section a little above the callus corresponds fully with fig. 9 b by Wittrock. In the monostromatic part of the frond the cells are ovale or vertically rectangular with rounded corners, seldom semicircular, 18—24 µ high and 6—15 µ broad. The chlorophyllous body occupies sometimes almost the whole cell, sometimes only a part of it, but, as far as I have seen, it never is disciform and horizontally rectangular. Cp. Wittr. l. c. p. 48, t. 3, fig. 9 d. Perhaps this difference at least partly derives from Wittrock's only having dried specimens for examination.

The form *Farlowii* is distinguished from the typical one by its thinner frond, being mostly cuneate-lanceolate, elongated-obovate or lanceolate, attenuated towards the base and more or less obtuse at the summit, — contrary to the shape of f. *typica*. It is less folded and the colour frequently paler than by the latter. The monostromatic part of the frond is 18—20 µ thick by Finmarkian specimens, and the structure similar to that of the typical form. Farlow certainly quotes *M. pulchrum* having a thickness of only 6 µ, but specimens from Nahant, Mass., communicated to me by Collins under the name of *M. pulchrum* are in the middle, monostromatic, part of the frond about 30 µ thick. Perhaps Farlow's measurment refers to the uppermost part of the frond, or the specimens have been younger.

The species in question is litoral (f. *typica* and f. *Far-*

lowii) and sublitoral (f. *Farlowii*). In the former case it grows on rocks and shells *(Mytilus)* or attached to other algæ, as *Rhodymenia palmata*, *Halosaccion ramentaceum* and *Gigartina mamillosa* in the lower part of the zone. In the latter case it has been found fastened to *Desmarestia aculeata* on a depth of 2—5 fathoms. It seems to occur only on open coast and to thrive best in much exposed localities. Specimens furnished with zoospores have been taken in July and August.

Distribution: Found at Kjöllefjord, pretty plentiful but local, Mehavn, rather scarce, and at Finkongkjeilen, scarce.

Monostroma saccodeum Kjellm.
N. Ish. Algfl. p. 365.

f. *typica*.
Descr. Monostroma saccodeum Kjellm. l. c.
Fig.   „   „   „   „   t. 28, fig. 1—10.

f. *cylindracea* Kjellm. (nob.)
Descr. Monostroma cylindreaceum Kjellm. l. c. p. 363.
Fig.   „   „   „   „   t. 30.

I have often met with *M. cylindraceum* but especially *M. saccodeum* along the coast of East-Finmarken as well as farther south, but I have been unable to find any real limit between them. I consequently consider them as different forms of the same species, regarding *M. saccodeum* the typical one.[1] I have even seen specimens of f. *cylindracea* which nearly approache *M. lubricum* Kjellm.

The present plant is litoral, growing in pools in the upper part of the zone, on stones, shells of Balanidæ, or fastened to other algæ, as *Fuci*, *Gigartina mamillosa*, *Rhodo*-

---

1. I want here to remark, that I some years ago probably have distributed *M. angicava* or another species under the name af *M. saccodeum*.

mela lycopodioides and *Halosaccion ramentaceum*. It occurs on open coasts as well as sheltered ones, and it attains a length of until 25 cm. Zoospore-bearing specimens have been collected in July and August.

Distribution: Apparently pretty common all along the coast and at some places abundant. I have taken it at Sværholt, common but not plentiful, Mehavn, local but abundant, Berlevaag and Vardö, rather scarce, Vadsö, rather scarce (f. *cylindracea*), and Pasvig, pretty plentiful.

Monostroma angicava Kjellm.

N. Ish. Algfl. p. 366.

Descr. Monostroma angicava Kjellm. l. c.

Fig. „ „ „ „ t. 29.

This is probably the most common *Monostroma* along the coast of East-Finmarken. It appears to be a well differentiated but much varying species. The plant has when young frequently the form of a pear-shaped bladder but is sometimes also cylindrical. A specimen in my collections has the form of a cylindrical sack, 8 cm. long and 1,5 cm. in diameter. Another is 18 cm. long and 3 cm. in diameter upwards, and open at the top. When it in its further growth bursts down to the base and expands membraneously, it often does not become laciniate but continues simple with, in general, slashed margin. A specimen is 18 cm. long and 18 cm. broad with deep reniform base. Another is 16 cm. long and 14 cm. broad with cordate base. Others have a broad, cuneate base. But, on the other hand, the frond is sometimes split up even to the base in broader or narrower segments, depending on the place of growth. When small, such specimens much remind of certain forms of *M. arcticum*.

The present species is litoral, growing on rocks, in rock-pools and attached to shells af Balanidæ or to other algæ, as *Fuci*, *Halosaccion ramentaceum*, *Gigartina mamillosa* and *Rhodymenia palmata*. It thrives best on open coast and rather exposed localities. I have collected specimens with zoospores in the later half of June and in July.

Distribution: Common and mostly plentiful all along the open coast.

Monostroma arcticum Wittr.
Monostr. p. 44.
Descr. Monostroma arcticum Wittr. l. c.
Fig. „   „   „   „ t. 2, fig. 8.
Exsicc. „   „ Wittr. et Nordst. Alg. exsicc. Nr. **144**.

By a cross section of the monostromatic part of the frond of this species, the cells are not always horizontally ovale, but sometimes roundish, vertically ovale, or even vertically rectangular with rounded corners. The plant is litoral, chiefly growing in rock-pools in the upper part of the zone, fastened to *Corallina officinalis* or other algæ, or attached to shells of Balanidæ. It seems to occur only on open coast. Specimens with zoospores have been taken in the later half of June, in July and in the first part of August.

Distribution: Pretty common along the open coast and at several places rather plentiful.

Monostroma fuscum (Post. et Rupr.) Wittr.
Monostr. p. 53; Ulva fusca Post. et Rupr. Ill. Alg. p. 21.
Descr. Monostroma fuscum Wittr. l. c.
Fig. „   „   „   „ t. 4, fig. 13.
Exsicc. Ulva sordida Aresch. Alg. Scand. exsicc. Nr. 120.
   Monostroma fuscum Wittr. et Nordst. Alg. exsicc. Nr. 143.
      „   „ Hauck et Richt. Phyc. univ. Nr. 124.
Syn. Ulva sordida Aresch. Phyc. Scand. p. 413.

This alga is, in general, sublitoral, occurring in the upper part of the zone, but sometimes also appearing in the lowermost part of the litoral zone, on open coasts as well as sheltered ones. It frequently grows on stones or shells. Specimens with zoospores have been taken in August.

Distribution: Pretty common and plentiful along the whole coast.

Monostroma Blyttii (Aresch.) Wittr.
Monostr. p. 49; Ulva Blyttii Aresch. in Fr. Summ. Veg. p. 129.
Descr. Monostroma Blyttii Wittr. l. c.
    „ „ Kleen, Nordl. Alg. p. 42.
Fig.   „ „ Kjellm. Spetsb. Thall. 2, t. 4, fig. 1—7.
Exsicc. „ „ Aresch. Alg. Scand. exsicc. Nr. 423.
    „ „ Wittr. et Nordst. Alg. exsicc. Nr. 44.
Syn. Ulva rigida Sommerf. Suppl. p. 185.

The species is chiefly litoral, living in rock-pools and fastened to shells *(Mytilus)* or other algæ, as *Corallina officinalis* and *Halosaccion ramentaceum*, on open as well as sheltered coasts. Zoospore-bearing specimens have been collected in July and August.

Distribution: Common and abundant almost everywhere.

Gen. Ulva (L.) Wittr.
Monostr. p. 9; L. Syst. Nat. Ed. 10, p. 1346.

Ulva lactuca L.
Spec. Plant. 2, p. 1163.
Descr. Ulva lactuca Born. et Thur. Etud. Phycol. p. 5.
Fig. „ „ „ „ t. 2—3.
Exsicc. „ „ Wittr. et Nordst. Alg. exsicc. Nr. 141.
Syn. Ulva latissima Kleen, Nordl. Alg. p. 40.

Litoral, occurring on rocks near low-vater mark. I have collected zoospore-bearing specimens in the beginning of August.

Distribution: Found only at Pasvig in Sydvaranger, rare.

Gen. Enteromorpha (Link) Harv.
Man. p. 173; Link. Epist. p. 5; ɔ parte,

Enteromorpha erecta (Lyngb.) J. G. Ag.

Alg. Syst. 3, p. 152; Scytosiphon erectus Lyngb. Hydr. Dan. p. 65.
Descr. Enteromorpha erecta J. G. Ag. l. c.
Fig. Scytosiphon erectus Lyngb. l. c. t. 15.

Ahlner has had the kindness to examine my collections of *Enteromorpha*. He has with doubt referred to the present species a couple of specimens from East-Finmarken. They grew in the litoral zone attached to *Halosaccion ramentaceum*.

Distribution: Only found at Sværholt, very rare.

Enteromorpha clathrata (Roth.) Grev.

Alg. Brit. p. 181; Conferva clathrata Roth, Cat. Bot. 3, p. 175.
Descr. Enteromorpha clathrata Ahln. Enterom. p. 43.
Exsicc. „ „ Wittr. et Nordst. Alg. exsicc. Nr. 130.

Litoral, growing on sandy localities, or in rock-pools at high-water mark, on open coasts as well as sheltered ones. It attains a length of about 35 cm., and it is furnished with zoospores in July.

Distribution: Apparently pretty common olong the whole coast. I have seen it at Kjöllefjord, Mehavn, Syltefjord (pretty plentiful), Vadsö (abundant), Bugönæs and Kjelmö in Sydvaranger.

Enteromorpha crinita (Roth) J. G. Ag.

Alg. Syst. 3, p. 144; Conferva crinita Roth, Cat. Bot. 1, p. 162.
Descr. Enteromorpha crinita J. G. Ag. l. c.
Fig. Conferva crinita Roth, l. c. t. 1, fig. 3.
Exsicc. Enteromorpha clathrata Aresch. Alg. Scand. exsicc. Nr. 328.

This species is litoral, fastened to *Halosaccion ramentaceum*. Specimens collected in the beginning of August were sterile.

Distribution: Found only at Sværholt, scarce.

Enteromorpha radiata J. G. Ag.

Alg. Syst. 3, p. 156.

Descr. Enteromorpha radiata J. G. Ag. l. c.
Fig.   „   „   „   „ t. 4, fig. 105—103.

Litoral, occurring on rocks at low-water mark, or in rock-pools in the upper part of the zone. I also found it cast on shore together with *Ptilota pectinata*, probably from the sublitoral zone. It appears to prefer exposed places. Specimens with zoospores have been collected at the end of June and in the beginning of July.

Distribution: Found at Sværholt, Mehavn and Finkongkjeilen, rare.

Enteromorpha intestinalis (L.) Link.
Epist. p. 5; Ulva intestinalis L. Spec. Pl. p. 1163.

f. *genuina* Ahln.
Enterom. p. 18.
Descr. Enteromorpha intestinalis α genuina Ahln. l. c.
         „   „   β clavata J. G. Ag. Alg. Syst. 3, p. 131
Fig.   „   „   Kütz. Tab. Phyc. 6, t. 31.
Exsicc. „   „   Aresch. Alg. Scand. exsicc. Nr. 122
          „   „   f. genuina Hauck et Richt. Phyc. univ. Nr. 223.

f. *attenuata* Ahln.
l. c. p. 20.
Descr. Enteromorpha intestinalis b. attenuata Ahln l. c.
         „   „   α cylindracea J. G. Ag. Alg. Syst. 3, p. 131.
Exsicc. „   „   f. longissima Aresch. Alg. Scand. exsicc. Nr. 327.
          „   „   f. attenuata Wittr. et Nordst. Alg. exsicc. Nr. 136.

f. *cornucopiæ* Lyngb.
Scytosiphon intestinalis γ cornucopiæ Lyngb. Hydr. Dan. p. 67.
Descr. Enteromorpha intestinalis c. cornucopiæ Ahln. l. c. p. 21.
         „   „   γ   „   J. G. Ag. l. c.
Exsicc. „   „   var. „   Wittr. et Nordst. Alg. exsicc. Nr. 137.

Exsicc. Enteromorpha intestinalis var. pumila Aresch Alg. Scand. exsicc. Nr. 268.
Syn. Ulva intestinalis Gunn. Fl. Norv. 2. p. 120.
„ compressa Wg. Fl. Lapp. p. 508; ex parte.
„ intestinalis Sommerf. Suppl. p. 186.

This species generally appears under the forms *attenuata* and *genuina*, yet the latter less common than the former. The form *cornucopiæ* I have only seen at Mehavn, Vardö and Vadsö. At the last mentioned place I met with a very slender form of f. *attenuata*. The present plant is litoral and lives on sandy localities, often at the mouths of streamlets, or on rocks and in rock-pools in the upper part of the zone, more seldom epiphytic on other algæ, as *Fuci*. It occurs on open as well as sheltered coasts. It has been collected with zoospores in June and July, at West-Finmarken also in August and September.

Distribution: Pretty common along the whole coast, at several places abundant, as Mehavn, Gamvik and Vadsö.

Enteromorpha compressa (L.) Ahln.
Enterom. p. 31; Ulva compressa L. Spec. Plant. p. 1163.

f. *typica*.
Descr. Enteromorpha compressa Ahln. l. c.
Fig. „ „ Kütz. Tab. Phyc. 6, t. 38.
Exsicc. „ „ Le Jol. Alg. mar. Cherb. Nr. 142.

f. *racemosa* Ahln.
l. c. p. 33.
Descr. Enteromorphe compressa c. racemosa Ahln. l. c.
Exsicc. „ ramulosa Aresch. Alg. Scand. exsicc. Nr. 226.
Syn. Ulva compressa Wg. Fl. Lapp. p. 508; ex parte.
„ „ Sommerf. Suppl. p. 186.

The form of f. *racemosa* I met with at East-Finmarken somewhat differs from the above quoted one distributed by Areschoug. The subelongated main-thread is densely clothed with long and almost capillary branches, which sometimes again bear some branch of second order. I have also met with a transition between this form and the typical one. Provisionally I refer to the present species a simple dark green *Enteromorpha*, which, with regard to the structure, differs rather much from *E. compressa*, such as the species is characterized by Ahlner.

The species in question occurs on rocks or in rockpools within the litoral region. Specimens collected in the middle of July were sterile.

Distribution: Found at Berlevaag, pretty plentiful but local, and at Kiberg, rather scarce.

Enteromorpha complanata Kütz.
Specc. Alg. p. 480; Cfr. Ahln. Enterom. p. 25.

f. *subsimplex* (Aresch.) Ahln.
l. c. p. 28; Enteromorpha compressa var. subsimplex Aresch. Alg. Scand. exsicc. Nr. 177.
Descr. Enteromorpha complanata var. subsimplex Ahln. l. c. p. 28.
Fig.   „   „   „   „   „   „ fig. 2 c.
Exsicc.   „   compressa   „   „   Aresch. Alg. Scand. exsicc. Nr 177.
Syn. Enteromorpha compressa α subsimplex J. G. Ag. Alg. Syst. 3, p. 137.

The Finmarkian specimens agree well with the above quoted form distributed by Areschoug. The plant becomes here until 60 cm. long. It grows in rock-pools or shallow sandy pools between tides. Specimens taken in July have been sterile.

Distribution: Found at Berlevaag and Mehavn, pretty plentiful.

Enteromorpha usneoides (Bonnem.) J. G. Ag.
Alg. Syst. 3, p. 157; Ulva usneoides Bonnem. sec. J. G. Ag. l. c.
Descr. Enteromorpha usneoides J. G. Ag. l. c.
           „   plumosa Ahln. l. c. p. 37.
Fig.   „   „   „   „   fig. 4.

Litoral, growing in rock-pools between tides.
Distribution: Only found at Sværholt, rare.

Enteromorpha micrococca Kütz.
Tab. Phyc. 6, p. 11.

f. *obconica* J. G. Ag.
Alg. Syst. 3, p. 123.

Descr. Enteromorpha micrococca α obconica J. G. Ag. l. c.

f. *tortuosa* J. G. Ag.
l. c.

Descr. Enteromorpha micrococca β tortuosa J. G. Ag. l. c.
Fig. „ „ Kütz. Tab. Phyc. 6, t. 30.
Syn. Enteromorpha micrococca Ahln. l. c. p. 46, fig. a. b.
Ulva intestinalis var. nana Sommerf. Suppl. p. 186.

This species is litoral and occurs on rocks or in clefts of rocks at high-water mark. It appears to prefer open and exposed coast, but it also is to be found in rather sheltered localities. At Kjelmö I met with very slender, almost thread-narrow specimens of f. *obconica*. This form becomes 10 cm. long. The plant has been taken with zoospores in the later half of August.

Distribution: Pretty common everywhere, except in the inner part of the deep fjords, and at some places abundant. The most common form is f. *tortuosa*.

Enteromorpha microphylla nob.
E. thallo simplici, vel inferne sparsim ramoso, utrinque attenuato, tubuloso-compresso, sæpe tortuoso, 20—25 μ crasso; cellulis 4—5—6 angularibus plus minusque seriatim ordinatis, in sectione transversale subquadratis vel rectangularibus. Tab. 2, fig. 10—16.

The name above is given provisionally, as I am not able to refer the species to any known form. It resembles *E. micrococca* in habit, but in structure it is plainly distinguished from that species. On the other hand it reminds of certain forms of *E. intestinalis*. It is a small plant, commonly 3—5 cm. long. The frond is until 5 mm. broad in the middle part, but in general much narrower, not seldom almost filiform, and from there partly attenuated downwards as well as upwards, partly rather obtuse at the summit. It is frequently simple, but sometimes it bears some few, short, simple and filiform branches in the lower part of the frond. In this part the cells are, seen from the surface, 4—5—6 angulated with rather sharp corners and ordered in more or less regular series. In the upper part the cells are smaller, often with more rounded corners and not seldom without any order. In a cross section they are squarish or vertically rectangular, mostly with rounded corners.

The species is litoral, occurring on rocks or in clefts of rocks at high-water mark. It has only been found on open coast. In the beginning of August it was furnished with zoospores.

Distribution: Found at Berlevaag and Havningberg, at both places scarce.

Enteromorpha tubulosa Kütz.
Tab. Phyc. 6, p. 11; E. intestinalis γ tubulosa Kütz. Spec. Alg. p. 478.
Descr. Enteromorpha tubulosa Ahln. l. c. p. 49; excl. var.
Fig.   "   "   Kütz. Tab. Phyc. 6, t. 32.
         "   "   Ahln. l. c. fig. 9.

Litoral, growing in rock-pools at high-water mark. Specimens with zoospores have been taken in July.

Distribution: Only found al Bugönæs in Sydvaranger, pretty plentiful but local.

Enteromorpha prolifera (Müll.) J. G. Ag.
Alg. Syst. 3, p. 129; Ulva prolifera Müll. Fl. Dan. t. 763, fig. 1.
Descr. Enteromorpha prolifera J. G. Ag. l. c.
         "   tubulosa b. pilifera Ahln. Enterom. p. 50.
Fig.   "   pilifera Kütz. Tab. Phyc. 6, t. 30.
         "   prolifera J. G. Ag. l. c. t. 4, fig. 103—104.

Exsicc. Enteromorpha tubulosa var. pilifera Wittr. et Nordst. Alg. ex sicc. Nr. 232.

I have only seen some few specimens of this species. They grew in rock-pools between tides, on open coast. The plant was steril when collected in the middle of August.

Distribution: Found only at Sværholt, rare.

Gen. **Diplonema** Kjellm.
N. Ish. Algfl. p. 371.

Diplonema confervoideum (Lyngb.) Rke.
Ostseefl. p. 80; Scytosiphon compressus Lyngb. Hydr. Dan. p. 65.
Deser. Diplonema percursum Kjellm. N. Ish. Algfl. p. 371.
Fig. Tetranema „ Aresch. Phyc. Scand. t. 2 A.
Schizogonium nodosum Kütz. Tab. Phyc. 6, t. 99.
percursum Kütz. l. c.
Enteromorpha percursa Kjellm. Algenv. Murm. Mee. t. 1, fig. 25.
Exsicc. Tetranema percursum Aresch. Alg. Scand. exsicc. Nr. 125.
Enteromorpha percursa Wittr. et Nordst. Alg. exsicc. Nr. 140.
Diplonema percursum „ „ „ „ „ 644.
Syn. Ulva percursa Sommerf. Suppl. p. 187.
Enteromorpha percursa J. G. Ag. Alg Syst. 3, p. 140; ex parte.
„ „ De Toni, Syll. Alg. 1, p. 129; ex parte.

The species is litoral, growing in pools in the upper part of the zone. At West-Finmarken, where I met with it in great abundance, I have seen transitions between the forms *typica* and *crassiuscula* Kjellm., and I think they hardly may be regarded as different forms. The few specimens that I have seen at East-Finmarken are most nearly to be related to the typical form. Cp. Kjellm. l. c.

Distributior: Found at Vardö, Kiberg and Bugönæs, very rare.

Fam. **Blastosporaceæ** Jess.
Monogr. p. 13.

Gen. **Prasiola** (Ag.) Jess.
l. c. Ag. Spec. Alg. **1**, p. 416; char. mut.

Prasiola furfuracea (Mert.) Menegh.
Cenni p. 36; Ulva furfuracea Mert. in Fl. Dan. t 1489.
Descr. Prasiola furfuracea Lagerst. Monogr. p. 31.
Fig.   „   „   Grev. Alg. Brit. t. 18.
  „   „   Jess. l. c. t. 2, fig. 1—10.
  „   „   Lagerst. l c. fig. 3.
Exsicc.   „   „   Aresch. Alg. Scand. exsicc. Nr. 221.
  „   „   Wittr. et Nordst. Alg. exsicc. Nr. 49, 438, 642.

At East-Finmarken I three times met with this species growing on rocks as far down on the sea-shore that it almost constantly was washed over by the waves, or at or a little above high-water mark, in the same hight as *Rhizoclonium riparium* and *Enteromorpha micrococca*. Cp. Wittr. et Nordst. Alg. exsicc. Nr. 642. Sometimes it grows side by side or even together with *P. stipitata.* Cp. Wittr. et Nordst. l. c. Nr. 435 and 438.

Distribution: Found at Mehavn, Vardö and Pasvig. I have also seen it at several other places, but at some distance from the shore.

Prasiola Lenormandiana Suhr
sec. Jess. Monogr. p. 17.
Descr. Prasiola leprosa Lagerst. Monogr. p. 33.
Fig.   „   „   Jess. Monogr. t. 2, fig. 17—23.
Exsicc.   „   „   Wittr. et Nordst. Alg. exsicc. Nr. 643.
Syn. Prasiola leprosa Rabenh. Fl. Eur. Alg. 3, p. 309; non. Kütz.

I agree with Lagerstedt (l. c.) regarding this plant a separate species. I at least never saw any transition to *P. furfuracea*, though it rather much reminds of that species. It is distinguished from the latter especially by its smallness and the shape of the frond, and it appears to me to be pretty well differentiated. As the description of *P. leprosa* Kütz. in Phyc. germ. and Spec. Alg. refers to *P. furfuracea*, and the figure in Tab. Phyc. 5, t. 39 is considered by J. G. A g a r d h (Alg. Syst. 3, p. 81) to belong to the last named species, I think it most correct to record the above quoted name, given to it by S u h r.

The species in question occurs on rocks on the sea-shore in exposed places, washed over by the waves. It grows gregarious in great numbers, sometimes clothing large spaces of the rocks. At West-Finmarken I also met with it at some distance from the shore.

Distribution: Found at the foot of the birds' rocks at Sværholt, abundant, and at Finkongkjeilen, scarce. I suppose it to be the same species I saw from the boot between Finkongkjeilen and Omgang on the foot of the birds' rocks in great abundance.

Prasiola stipitata Suhr
in Jess. Monogr. p. 16.

Descr. Prasiola stipitata Lagerst. Monogr. p. 36.
Fig. „   „   Jess. Monogr. t. 2, fig. 11—16.
Exsicc. „   „   Wittr. et Nordst. Alg. exsicc. Nr. 48 et 435.
         „   „   Aresch. Alg. Scand. exsicc. Nr. 138 et 222.

This species occurs on rocks on the sea-shore and often so far down that it is constantly washed over by the waves. At Bugönæs in Sydvaranger I met with a very small form most nearly related to the present species growing in a small and shallow rock-pool or cleft of rock at high-water mark.

Distribution: Pretty common but not plentiful along the whole coast.

Gen. **Schizogonium** Kütz.
Phyc. gener. p. 245.

Schizogonium radicans (Kütz.) Gay.
Ulothr. aér., sec. Notarisia 1888, p. 566; Ulothrix radicans Kütz.

Spec. Alg. p. 349.
Descr. Schizogonium radicans Gay l. c.
  Ulothrix discifera Kjellm. Spetsb. Thall. 2, p. 52.
Fig.   „   radicans Kütz. Tab. Phyc. 2, t. 95.
    „   discifera Kjellm. l. c. t. 5, fig. 10—14.
  Syn. Hormidium murale De-Toni, Syll. Alg. 1, p. 156; ex parte fide syn.

In the eastern part of the district I met with a *Schizogonium* which no doubt is identic with *Ulothrix radicans* Kütz. It corresponds well with fig. a. a′. a″. and b. c. e. in Kütz. Tab. Phyc. l. c. This plant is considered by De-Toni to belong to *Hormidium murale*. I agree with Gay as to the limitation of the latter, and keep *Schiz. radicans* a distinct species. On the other hand, the Finmarkian specimens fully coincide with *Ulothrix discifera* Kjellm. in shape as well as thickness. Individuals which exactly resemble the figures by Kjellman l. c., except fig. 12, were common together with other resembling the figures by Kützing, and without any limit between them. Sometimes two threads are grown together.

The present plant occurs on rocks at or a little above high-water mark, on exposed coast. It forms rather thin but densely interwoven strata, mostly with rough or undulate-lacunosed surface. It also grows in small number together with other smaller algæ on rocks between tides.

Distribution: Found at Hornö on Vardö, local but pretty plentiful, and in two localities at Vardö together with *Calothrix* and other algæ, scarce.

Fam. **Cladophoraceæ** (Hass.) Wittr.

Pitoph. p. 42; Hass. Brit. Freshw. Alg.; lim. mut.

Gen. **Spongomorpha** Kütz.

Phyc. gener. p. 275.

Spongomorpha spinescens Kütz.

Spec. Alg. p. 418.
Descr. Spongomorpha spinescens Kütz. l. c.
    „   „   Kjellm. N. Ish. Algfl. p. 373.
Fig.   „   „   „ Tab. Phyc. 4, t. 75.
Exsicc. „   „ Wittr. et Nordst. Alg. exsicc. Nr. 115.

The common form of this species is that one described by Kjellman l. c., forming «very dense, usually perfectly spherical, or flattened spherical balls of light-green colour, composed of obpyramedical clusters with truncate tops». Besides I also met with a form composed of looser clusters, resembling certain forms of *S. arcta*, and sometimes approaching this species also with reference to the ramification. However it appears to be a pretty well marked species. It is smaller than *S. arcta*, being in general 3—4 cm. long, sometimes attaining 8 cm.

The species is litoral and occurs only at exposed places, epiphytic on *Gigartina mamillosa* in the lower part of the zone. A few specimens were found on rocks together with *S. arcta*. It is furnished with zoospores in August.

Distribution: Found at Sværholt and Vardö, local but abundant.

Spongomorpha arcta (Dillw.) Kütz.

Spec. Alg. p. 417; Conferva arcta Dillw. Brit. Conf. Suppl. p. 67.

f. *pulvinata* Fosl.
in Wittr. et Nordst. Alg. exsicc. Nr. 614.

f. *typica* Fosl.
in Wittr. et Nordst. Alg. exsicc. Nr. 612.

Descr. Conferva arcta Aresch. Phyc. Scand. p. 426.
Fig. Cladophora arcta Harv. Phyc. Brit. t. 135.
    „   vaucheriæformis Kütz. Tab. Phyc. 3, t. 78.
    „   comosa Kütz. l. c. t. 79.
    „   stricta Kütz. l. c. t. 80.
  Spongomorpha arcta Kütz. Tab. Phyc. 4, t. 74.
    „   cymosa Kütz. l. c. t. 74.

Spongomorpha centralis Kütz. 1. c. t. 80.
Exsicc. Conferva arcta Aresch. Alg. Scand. exsicc. Nr. 129.
Cladophora arcta Aresch. l. c. Nr. 334 et 335.
Spongomorpha arcta Wittr. et Nordst. Alg. exsicc. Nr. 114, 316, 413, 612.
Conferva centralis Wyatt, Alg. Danm. Nr. 46.

f. *penicilliformis* Fosl.
in Wittr. et Nordst. Alg. exsicc. Nr. 613.

f. *Sonderi* Kütz. (nob.)
Spec. Alg. p. 419.
Descr. Spongomorpha Sonderi Hauck, Meeresalg. p. 444.
Fig.   „   „   Kütz. Tab. Phyc. 4, p. 79.

f. *hystrix* Strömf. (nob.)
Descr. Spongomorpha hystrix Strömf. Isl. Algveg. p. 54.
  Syn. Conferva arcta Lyngb. Hydr. Dan. p. 157.
    „   centralis Lyngb. l. c. p. 161.

I have taken the above mentioned typical form in a rather wide sense. Probably it may be divided into two subforms, α *stricta* and β *centralis*. Most nearly related to it is, on the one side, the form that I have distributed in Wittr. et Nordst. Alg. exsicc. Nr. 614 under the name of f. *pulvinata*. It is easely recognized by its mode of growth, and very numerous rhizoids connecting the particular branch-systems into dense masses. It often forms coherent mats spreading widely over sandcovered rocks. I have seen such mats several hundred square foot in extent by a thickness of 4—8 cm., and the surface sometimes almost plain. On the other side, the form *penicilliformis* is characterized by its penicillated or thinly clustered frond, the branches being erect and rather rigid, in the lower part of the frond loosely connected by numerous rhizoids. The main axis is at the base usually thinner than higher up, in the middle 100—140 µ thick, and chiefly upwards bearing pretty few elongated, erect branches. The cells are generally 1—2 times more long than thick. The rhizoids, by this form only appearing in the lower or lowest part of the frond, are long and branched, with the cells 40—60 µ thick and their length 5—9 times the thickness. To the present species I also refer *S. Sonderi* Kütz., characterized by its proportionate coarseness and rigidity, short cells and fastigiate outline. By the kindness of Ferd. Hauck I have had the opportunity to examine an authentic specimen of *S. Sonderi*, and to my experience it no doubt may be regarded a form af *S. arcta*. I also met with it at Finmarken. It closely resembles certain forms of f. *typica*, differing only with reference to its coarseness and rigidity, in which respects it reminds of f. *penicilliformis*. A still coarser form is *S. hystrix* Strömf., formerly only known from Iceland. According to Strömfelt (l. c.) it occurs on the coast of Iceland in ball-shaped specimens floating in the surface of the water, attaining a diameter of 10 cm. At the coast of Finmarken I found it lying loose on the bottom, forming loosely entangled masses of indefinate shape. However I have collected perfectly spherical balls of *S. arcta*, most nearly related to the typical form. The Finmarkian specimens of f. *hystrix* are sparingly branched with a thickness of about 200 µ, and the length of the cells varies between $^{1}/_{2}$ and 3 times the diameter.

The species in question is litoral and sublitoral. In the former case it grows on rocks, wood-works, in rock-pools, or epiphytic on other algæ in every part of the zone. In the latter case it descends to a depth of about 10 fathoms, occurring on various bottom, either fastened to stones or epiphytic on other algæ, even the leaves of *Laminaria digitata*. It partly appears scattered partly gregarious, and not seldom in large masses so as to give the vegetation its character. It occurs both on open and sheltered coasts, in much exposed as well as sheltered localites. The typical form lives in both the named regions; f. *pulvinata* I have only seen in the litoral zone, on open coast; f. *penicillifor-*

mis in rock-pools in the upper part of the named zone; f. *Sonderi* in the lowermost part of the litoral and uppermost part of the sublitoral regions, descending to a depth of about 4 fathoms; and f. *hystrix* sublitoral, on a depth of 2—8 fathoms. Specimens with zoospores have been collected in June, but sparingly.

Distribution: Common and abundant everywhere (f. *typica*). The form *pulvinata* only along the open coast, at most places plentiful; f. *penicilliformis* only found at Berlevaag, scarce; f. *Sonderi* at Mehavn, local but pretty plentiful; and f. *hystrix* at Kjöllefjord, rare. (The latter also found at West-Finmarken in rather great numbers).

Spongomorpha intermedia Fosl.
in Wittr. et Nordst. Alg. exsicc. Nr. 615.
Descr. Spongomorpha intermedia Fosl. l. c.

This species approaches on the one side to *S. arcta* (f. *pulvinata*) and on the other side to *S. atrovirens*. Cp. Wittr. et Nordst. Alg. exsicc. Nr. 616. But it is distinguished from both by essential characteristics.

The plant lives in rock-pools in the upper part of the litoral region at exposed places. I do not know when it develops its reproductive organs. Specimens collected in July were sterile.

Distribution: Found at Kiberg and Pasvig, local but pretty plentiful.

Spongomorpha lanosa (Roth) Kütz.
Spec. Alg. p. 420; Conferva lanosa Roth, Cat. Bot. 3, p. 291.

f. *typica*.
Descr. Cladophora lanosa Harv. Phyc. Brit. t. 6.
Fig. Spongomorpha lanosa Kütz. Tab. Phyc. 4, t. 83.
     „   villosa Kütz. l. c. t. 83.
     „   senescens Kütz. l. c. t. 84.
Cladophora lanosa Harv. Phyc. Brit. t. 6.
Exsicc. Conferva lanosa Aresch. Alg. Scand. exsicc. Nr. 181 et 228,

Spongomorpha lanosa f. villosa Fosl. in Wittr. et Nordst. Alg. exsicc. Nr. 611.

f. *uncialis* Fl. Dan. (Thur.)
in Le Jol Liste Alg. Cherb. p. 63; Conferva uncialis Fl. Dan. t. 771.
Descr. Cladophora uncialis Harv. Phyc. Brit. t. 207.
Fig. Spongomorpha uncialis Kütz. Tab. Phyc. 4, t. 80 et 82.
Cladophora uncialis Harv. Phyc. Brit. t. 207.
Exsicc. Conferva uncialis Aresch. Alg. Scand. exsicc. Nr. 130.
Spongomorpha uncialis Wittr. et Nordst. Alg. exsicc. Nr. 116 et 925.
Syn. Conferva uncialis Lyngb. Hydr. Dan. p. 60.
„ „ Sommerf. Suppl. p. 196.

The typical form is litoral, growing epiphytic on other algæ, as *Polyides rotundus, Cystoclonium purpurascens, Ceramium rubrum, Corall. officinalis* and *Chætopt. plumosa*. The form *uncialis* occurs in rock-pools between tides and in the uppermost part of the sublitoral zone. The plant has been collected with zoospores in development in the beginning of August. At West-Finmarken it has been taken with such organs at the end of May, and in August and September.

Distribution: The typical form found at Mehavn, Syltefjord and Kjelmö, rather scarce; f. *uncialis* at Lebesby, rather scarce, and at Kjelmö in Sydvaranger, local but pretty plentiful.

Spongomorpha minima Fosl.
in Tromsö Mus. Aarsh. X. p. 185.
Descr. Spongomorpha minima Fosl. l. c.
Fig. „ „ „ „ t. 3, f. 6.
Exsicc. „ „ Wittr. et Nordst. Alg. exsicc. Nr. 926.

This species seems to be nearly related to *S. lanosa*, and perhaps the plant later will prove to belong to the named species. However it is smaller, more flaccid and the cells remarkably thinner than by *S. lanosa*. There is also some difference with regard to the ramification, but I do not know yet whether constant.

The present plant is litoral and grows in rock-pools at high-water mark attached to *Cladophora rupestris* f. *submarina*. Specimens collected in July were sterile.

Distribution: Found only at Pasvig in Sydvaranger, rare.

Gen. Cladophora Kütz.
Phyc. gener. p. 262.

Cladophora rupestris (L.) Kütz.
Phyc. gener. p. 270; Conferva rupestris L. Spec. Pl. p. 1167.

f. *typica.*
Descr. Cladophora rupestris Harv. Phyc. Brit. t. 180.
Fig.   "   "   Kütz. Tab. Phyc. 4, t. 3.
     "   "   Harv. l. c.
Exsicc. Conferva   "   Aresch. Alg. Scand. exsicc. Nr. 126 et 269.
     Cladophora   "   Wittr. et Nordst. Alg. exsicc. Nr. 117.
     "   "   f. typica Wittr. et Nordst. l. c. Nr. 618 et 927.

f. *submarina* Fosl.
in Wittr. et Nordst. Alg. exsicc. Nr. 619.
Descr. Cladophora rupestis f. submarina Fosl. l. c.
Exsicc.   "   "   "   "   "   et Nr. 928.
Syn. Conferva rupestris Wg. Fl. Lapp. p. 512.
     "   "   Lyngb. Hydr. Dan. p. 156.
     "   "   Sommerf. in Act. Nidros. p. 27.

This alga at the coast of East-Finmarken never grows so luxuriant as farther south. It attains a length of about 12 cm. but it is in general much smaller. The typical form lives on rocks or in rocks-pools in the lower part of the zone, mostly at low-water mark, and f. *submarina* in brackwater-pools at or a little above high-water mark. The plant thrives best on open coast, and it bears zoospores in August. At Nordland I have taken zoospore-specimens in the beginning of March.

Distribution: Commonly spread along the whole coast; at some places, for inst. Sværholt and Vardö, pretty common but not plentiful. The form *submarina* found at Kirkenæs, Kjelmö and Pasvig ind Sydvaranger.

Cladophora Hutchinsiae (Dillw.) Kütz.
Phyc. germ. p. 210; Conferva diffusa Dillw. Brit. Conf. t. 109.
f. *distans* Kütz.
Spec. Alg. p. 392
Descr. Cladophora Hutchinsiae β distans Hauck, Meeresalg p. 453.
Fig.   „   diffusa Kütz. Tab. Phyc. 3, t. 88.
       „   „   Harv. Phyc. Brit. t. 130.

A litoral alga, accurring on rocks, stones or woodwork at extreme low-water mark. It probably also descends into the sublitoral zone. I have collected specimens with zoospores in the later half of July and in the beginning of August.

Distribution: Found at Sværholt, Kjöllefjord, Berlevaag, Havningberg and Vardö, everywhere scarce.

Cladophora glaucescens (Griff.) Harv.
Phyc. Brit. t. 196; Conferva glaucescens Griff. in Harv. Man. p. 139.
Descr. Cladophora glaucescens Harv. l. c.
Fig.   „   „   Kütz. Tab. Phyc. 4, t. 24.
      „   „   Harv. l. c.
Exsicc. Conferva   „   Wyatt, Alg. Danm. Nr. 195.
      Cladophora hirta β borealis Fosl. in Wittr. et Nordst. Alg exsicc. Nr. 621.
      „   glaucescens Fosl. in Wittr. et Nordst. l. c. Nr. 931.
Syn. Conferva glomerata β marina Wg. Fl. Lapp. p. 513.
     Cladophora sericea Kleen, Nordl. Alg. p. 45.,

Having had the opportunity to examine a considerable numbers of this species from different places, I am obliged to consider the above quoted plant distributed in W i t t r. et N o r d s t. Alg. exsicc. Nr. 621 under the name of *Cl. hirta* f. *borealis* only a form of the present species. It differs from typical specimens chiefly by its darker colour, greater rigidity, coarseness, shorter cells and thicker cell-walls, but I have seen almost every transition, and it appears to be so nearly related to the latter that it hardly may be regarded even a named form of the species. The present plant is rather much variable. I have seen specimens even still slender than that one distributed in Wyatt, Alg. Danm. l. c., though the Finmarkian specimens appear, in general, to be coarser than the British ones.

The species in question is litoral, occurring in pools in the upper part of the region. It thrives best on open coast but is also to be met with in sheltered localities, attaining a length of until 80 cm., and it is furnished with zoospores in the later half of July and in August.

Distribution: Pretty common and at several places rather plentiful especially along the open coast.

Cladophora gracilis (Griff.) Harv.
Phyc. Brit. t. 18; Conferva gracilis Griff. in Wyatt, Alg. Danm. Nr. 97.

Descr. Cladophora gracilis Farl. New. Engl. Alg. p. 55.
          „   „   Harv. l. c.
Fig.   „   „   Kütz. Tab. Phyc. 4, t. 23.
          „   „   Harv. l. c.
          „   vadorum Kütz. l. c. t. 20.

Exsicc. Conferva gracilis Wyatt, Alg. Danm. Nr. 97.
       Cladophora glaucescens Fosl. in Wittr. et Nordst. Alg. exsicc. Nr. 620.

Syn. Cladophora gracilis f. borealis Fosl. herb.

This is a still more varying species than the preceding one. There is a great difference between the specimen distributed in Wyatt, Alg. Danm. l. c. and the northern form that appears in exposed localities along the coast of Finmarken, and, if numerous transitions were not seen, they would hardly be thought to belong to the same species. The latter is smaller, usually 4—6 cm. long, of a rather dark green colour, robust, densely branched, sometimes forming roundish balls, and in the lower part of the frond often very coarse with thick cell-wals. I have distributed this form under the name of *Cl. gracilis f. borealis*. But as yet I am uncertain whether it may be regarded more than a local variety of the species. The plant is generally smaller along the northern coast of Norway than more south. However I have seen British specimens determined by Harvey which almost fully coincide with Finmarkian ones of the normal form. On the other hand the species sometimes approaches nearley to *Cl. glaucescens*. Cp. Wittr. et Nordst. Alg. exsicc. Nr. 620.

The present species is litoral and grows in pools in the upper part of the zone. It occurs both on open and sheltered coasts, but it seems to prefer protected places. Specimens with zoospores have been collected in August.

Distribution: Pretty common along the whole coast and at serveral places plentiful.

Gen. Rhizoclonium Kütz.
Phyc gener. p. 261.

Rhizoclonium riparium (Roth) Harv.
Phyc. Brit. t. 238; Conferva riparia Roth, Cat. Bot. 3, p. 216.

f. *typica* Wittr.
in Wittr. et Nordst. Alg. exsicc. Nr. 623.
Descr. Rhizoclonium riparium f. typica Wittr. l. c.
Fig. „ „ Harv. Phyc. Brit. t. 238.
Exsicc. „ „ Wittr. et Nordst. l. c.
Cfr. Conferva implexa Aresch. Alg. Scand. exsicc. Nr. 136.

f. *valida* Fosl.
in Wittr. et Nordst. Alg. exsicc. Nr. 624.
Descr. Rhizoclonium riparium f. valida Fosl. l. c.

f. *pannosa* (Aresch.) nob.
Conferva pannosa Aresch. Alg. Scand. exsicc. Ser. 1, Nr. 16.
Descr. Rhizoclonium pannosum Kütz. Spec. Alg. p. 384.
Conferva implexa *b.* Aresch. Phyc. Scand. p. 434: excl. syn. plur.
Fig. Rhizoclonium pannosum Kütz. Tab Phyc. 3, t. 70 I.
Exsicc. Conferva pannosa Aresch. l. c.
Syn. Conferva obtusangula Lyngb. Hydr. Dan. p. 159.
„   „   Sommerf. Suppl. p. 195.

The typical form of this species forms thin but often extensive strata on rocks, in shallow clefts of rocks, or in the margin of rock-pools, sometimes together with other species, as *Cladophora*, *Spongomorpha* and *Rhodochorton Rothii*. It is in general less curved and has fewer rhizoid branches than the form figured by Harvey in Phyc. Brit. l. c., but I have seen specimens which fully correspond with the quoted figure. The form distributed by Areschoug in Alg. Scand. exsicc. Nr. 136 appears to be a transition between *f. typica* and *f. tenuior* Wittr. et Nordst. Alg. exsicc. Nr. 625, though most nearly related to the former. The form that I have called *f. valida* is distinguished from the typical one chiefly by its coarseness and mode of growth. It occurs in narrow and somewath deep clefts of exposed rocks, forming rough, crispate-elevated cushions. The threads differ between 26 and 45 µ in thickness, usually about 30 µ. A form very unlike the latter in habit but otherwise nearly related to it is the above mentioned *f. pannosa* It grows on posts or other woodwork, or sometimes on rocks, and forms rather thick and dense layers with a undulate-lacunosed surface. In coarseness and the length of the cells it corresponds with f *valida*, but the rhizoid branches are numerous and longer than by the latter.

The present plant lives in the upper part of the litoral zone, sometimes even a little above high-water mark, on open coasts as well as sheltered ones. Specimens with zoospores have been collected in the later half of June, in July and August. At Tromsö I have taken such ones in October (*f. pannosa*).

Distribution: Common and pretty plentiful almost everywhere, at some places, for. inst. Mehavn, abundant *(f. typica)*. The form *valida* is rather scarce, and *f. pannosa* has not been found at East-Finmarken but at West-Finmarken and in Tromsö amt.

Rhizoclonium rigidum Gobi
Algenfl. Weiss. Meer. p. 85.
Descr. Rhizoclonium rigidum Gobi, l. c.
Exsicc. Conferva fracta f. longissima subsimplex Aresch. Alg. Scand. exsicc. Nr. 273.
Rhizoclonium rigidum Wittr. et Nordst. Alg. exsicc. Nr. 626.
Cfr. Conferva implexa Wyatt, Alg. Danm. Nr. 142.
Syn. Cladophora fracta Kleen, Nordl. Alg. p. 45.

This species is sometimes, especially in the state bearing reproductive organs, somewhat curled and twisted. I have specimens collected at East-Finmarken which almost fully correspond with *Conferva implexa* Wyatt, Alg. Danm. Nr. 142 even in thickness (25—36 µ). But the latter is by Le Jolis in Liste Alg. Cherb. p. 58 referred to *Rh. tortuosum*. To my opinion it does not belong to the last named species, being so nearly related to *Rh. rigidum* that no limit hardly may be drawn between them, and I do not think the two species may be united. *Conferva tortuosa* Wyatt l. c. Nr 190, which is a *Rhizoclonium*, more reminds of *Rh. tortuosum*, but it is more slender than the common form of this species. *Rh. rigidum* has in general, as far a I have seen, a thickness of 18—25 µ. However the specimens distributed by Areschoug l. c. is coarser, about 25—35 µ thick. *Rh. tortuosum* is a smaller plant, has a dark green colour, the threads are 30—45 µ (or, according to Farlow, 35—58 µ) thick, and much curled and twisted even in a younger state. I take *Rh. tortuosum* in the same sense as described by F a r l o w in New Engl. Alg. p. 49, and American, British and Norwegian specimens (the latter collected at Kristiansund) coincide fully with one another.

The species in question is litoral. It is at first attached to other algæ but afterwards forming prostrate strata of conciderable extent, or interwoven tufts among the branches of other algæ. At East-Finmarken I have only met with it in rock-pools between tides together with *Cladophora gracilis*, but at West-Finmarken I have seen it clothing the bottom from about half tide till about 2 fathoms below low-water mark and nearly the same extent in breadth, or some thousand square foot. (Wittr. et Nordst. Alg. exsicc. l. c.). The plant appears on open as well as sheltered coasts, but it seems to prefer sheltered places. It is furnished with zoospores in the later half of June and in August.

Distribution: Probably pretty common along the whole coast. I have seen it at Syltefjord, Vardö, Kiberg and Pasvig, somewhat local but plentiful.

Gen. **Chætomorpha** Kütz.
Phyc. germ. p. 203.

Chætomorpha melagonium (Web. et Mohr) Kütz.
l. c. p. 204; Conferva melagonium Web. et Mohr. Reise, p. 194.

f. *typica*.

Descr. Conferva melagonium Web. et Mohr. l. c.
Fig. Chætomorpha Picquotiana Kütz. Tab. Phyc. 3, t. 58.
Exsicc. „ melagonium Wittr. et Nordst. Alg. exsicc. Nr. 415.

f. *rupincola* Aresch.

Conferva melagonium var. rupincola Aresch. Alg. Scand. exsicc. Nr. 245 a.
Descr. Conferva melagonium Harv. Phyc. Brit. t. 99, A.
Fig. Chætomorpha melagonium Kütz. Tab. Phyc. 3, t. 61.

Exsicc. Conferva melagonium var. rupincola Aresch. l. c.
   Chætomorpha melagonium f. rupincola Wittr. et Nordst. Alg.
      exsicc. Nr. 632.
   Syn. Conferva melagonium Lyngb. Hydr. Dan. p. 148.

The typical form is sublitoral, growing on a depth of 3—8 fathoms, f. *rupincola* litoral, growing in rock-pools or on sand-covered rocks in the lower part of the zone. The latter sometimes appears gregarious in considerable numbers, and seems to prefer open coast. At East-Finmarken I only met with sterile specimens (in July and the earlier half of August), but at West-Finmarken the plant has been collected with zoospores at the end of May and in July.

Distribution: Generally scattered and very scarce along the whole coast, in a single place (Havningberg) abundant but local (f. *rupincola*). The typical form only found at Sværholt.

Chætomorpha tortuosa (Dillw.) Kütz.

Spec. Alg. p. 373; Conferva tortuosa Dillw. Brit. Conf. Syn. p. 46.
Descr. Conferva tortuosa Aresch. Phyc. Scand. p. 433.
   Chætomorpha tortuosa Hauck, Meeresalg. p. 439.
Fig. Conferva tortuòsa Aresch. Phyc. Scand. t. 3, G.
   Chætomorpha tortuosa Küt. Tab. Phyc. 3, t. 51.
   „   Callithrix Kütz. l. c. t. 51.
   Spongiopsis mediterranea Kutz. l. c. t. 50.
Exsicc. Conferva tortuosa Aresch. Alg. Scand. exsicc. Nr. 29.

The form of this species which appears along the coast of Finmarken forms loosely entangled masses, lying loose on the bottom, or floating on the surface of the water in pools or lagoons between tides. It agrees pretty well with the specimen distributed by Areschoug l. c. Yet the colour is a little paler. It is hardly possible to draw any limit between this form and the form described by Hauck l. c., the latter being very much curled and twisted, and having a dark green colour, much reminding of certain forms of *Rhizoclonium tortuosum*. A specimen communicated to me by H a u c k, in habit greatly resembles *Conferva tortuosa* Wyatt, Alg. Danm. Nr. 190, but, as I have stated before, the latter is a *Rhizoclonium*, probably a form of *Rh. tortuosum*. I have seen specimens from the southern Norway which almost fully coincide with Adriatic ones, and also transitions between the named forms.

The present species, on the coast of Finmarken, has only been found in sheltered localities, in the inner part of deep bays. Specimens collected in the beginning of July were sterile.

Distribution: Found at Kirkenæs in Sydvaranger, local but pretty plentiful.

Fam. Ulothrichaceæ (Rabenh.)
Flor. Eur. Alg. 3, p. 360; excl. Schizogonium, Hormidium.

Gen. Ulothrix Kütz.
Alg. Dec. Nr. 144; sec. Spec. Alg. p. 345.

U l o t h r i x i m p l e x a Kütz.
Spec. Alg. p. 349.
Descr. Ulothrix implexa Hauck, Meeresalg. p. 440.
Fig.   „   „   „   „   fig. 193.
         „   „   Kütz. Tab. Phyc. 2, t. 94.
         „   submarina Kütz. l. c.
Exsicc. „   implexa Hauck et Richt. Phyc. univ. Nr. 72.

This plant is at first fastened to other algæ, but afterwards is getting loose, forming tangled masses. I met with it fastened to *Dictyosiphon hippuroides* and *Cladophora gracilis*, or loosely entangled with the latter and *Rhizoclonium rigidum*, or jointly with other algæ. It is chiefly litoral and is frequently met with in rock-pools, on open as well as sheltered coasts. Once I found it in the uppermost part of the sublitoral zone together with *Antithamnion floccosum*. The Finmarkian specimens are 10—12 μ thick, bearing zoospores at East-Finmarken in the later half of July and in the first part of August, at West-Finmarken in the middle of June, and in Tromsö amt at the beginning of June.

Distribution: Pretty common along the whole coast and in several places rather plentiful.

Ulothrix flacca (Dillw.) Thur.
in Le Jol. Liste Alg. Cherb. p. 36; Conferva flacca Dillv. Brit. Conf. t. 49.

Descr. Ulothrix flacca Hauck, Meeresalg. p. 442.
„ „ Farl. New Engl. Alg. p. 45.
Fig. Hormotrichum flaccum Kütz. Tab. Phyc. 3, t. 63.
„ didymum Kütz. l. c.
Ulothrix flacca Tab. nostr. 3, fig. 1—3.

Exsicc. Lyngbya Carmichaelii Wyatt, Alg. Danm. Nr. 230.
Hormiscia flacca Aresch. Alg. Scand. exsicc. Nr. 342.

Syn. Lyngbya Carmichaelii Harv. Phyc. Brit. t. 186, A.; fide cit.
Urospora penicilliformis Aresch Obs. Phyc. 2, p. 4; ex parte.
„ „ Kjellm. N. Isl. Algfl. p. 386; ex parte.
Lyngbya flacca Harv. l. c. t. 300.

I agree with Farlow and Hauck considering the present plant a pretty well differentiated species. Along the coast of northern Norway at the least it is easely recognized, except in a younger state, when it is difficult to distinguish this species from young specimens of *Urospora penicilliformis*. Sometimes two threads are grown together, and now and then the plant bears very short, attenuated, simple branches, which are thinner than their main axis. The cells are often unequal in length in transverse direction of the frond, and often also varying in shape, reminding of certain forms of *Schizogonium radicans*. Cp. Kjellm. Spetsb. Thall. 2, t. 5, fig. 10—11. Sometimes they are very short in longitudinal direction of the frond, and the zoosporiferous ones are varying rather much in shape even in the same thread. Cp. t. 2, fig. 17—19. Perhaps the species, in the sense here taken, includes two different forms.

The species in question is litoral, and grows on woodwork or epiphytic on *Fucaceæ*. Once I met with it attached to *Rhodymenia palmata*. It also occurs on rocks at highwater mark, especially in localities where small freshwater-streams are moistening the rock. Specimens with zoospores have been collected in August.

Disribution: Found at Sværholt, Kjöllefjord and Vardö, rather scarce, and at Pasvig and Smaaströmmen in Sydvaranger, local but pretty plentiful.

Fam. Confervaceæ (Bonnem.) Lagerh.
in Ber. Deutsch. bot. Ges. Bd. 5, p. 409; Bonnem. in Journ. Phyc. XCIV, p. 193; lim. mut.

Gen. Urospora Aresch.
Obs. Phyc. 1, p. 15.

Urospora penicilliformis (Roth) Aresch.
Obs. Phyc. 2, p. 4; Conferva penicilliformis Roth. Cat. Bot. 3, p. 271.

Descr. Urospora penicilliformis Aresch. l. c.; excl. syn. plur.
Ulothrix isogona Farl. New. Engl. Alg. p. 45.

Fig. Hormotrichum penicilliforme Kütz. Tab. Phyc. 3, t. 64.
    a   vermiculare Kütz. l. c.
    „   isogonum Kütz. l. c. t. 65.
    „   Younganum Kütz. l. c.
Lyngbya speciosa Harv. Phyc. Brit. t. 186, B.
Conferva Youngana Harv. l. c. t. 328.

Exsicc. Lyngbya speciosa Wyatt, Alg. Danm. Nr. 196.
    Conferva speciosa Aresch. Alg. Scand. exsicc. Nr. 132 et 185.
    „   hormoides Aresch. l. c. Nr. 133 et 186.
Urospora mirabilis Aresch. l. c. Nr. 340.
    „   penicilliformis Wittr. et Nordst. Alg. exsicc. Nr. 417 et 418.

Syn. Urospora penicilliformis Kjellm. N. Ish. Algfl. p. 386; ex parte.

A litoral alga, growing on stones, rocks, wood-work, or epiphytic on other algæ, as *Fucaccæ* and *Halosaccion ramentaceum*. It appears gregarious and not seldom in great masses, so as to determine essentially the character of the vegetation, for inst. at Sværholt (Vestersiden), Kjöllefjord and Finkongkjeilen, and occurs both on open and sheltered coasts. Specimens furnished with zoospores have been collected in June, July and August.

Distribution: Common and abundant in most places along the whole coast, but somewhat local.

Fam. **Chroolepediaceæ** (Rabenh.) Borzi.
Studi alg. 1, p. 25; Rabenh. Fl. Eur. Alg. 3, p. 371; lim. mut.

Gen. Pilinia Kütz.
Phyc. gener. p. 273.

Pilinia minor Hansg.
in lit.

„Lager dünnhäutig, oder fast krustenförmig, gelblichgrün, mehr oder weniger ausgebreitet. Fäden meist kurz und wenig verzweigt. Wegetative Zellen 3 bis 5 μ breit, 1 bis 2 mal so lang, Endzellen abgerundet; in jeder Zelle ein wandständiger, bandförmiger Chlorophyllträger. Geht auch in einen einzelligen Protococcus-artigen Entwickelungszustand über". Tab. 2, fig. 17—22.

The species occurs on rocks and wood-work at high-water mark in exposed localities. It often appears gregarious together with *Lyngbya jadertina*, and sometimes also together with *Ulothrix flacca*.

Distribution: Found at Sværholt and Vardö, rather scarce.

Fam. Chætophoraceæ (Harv.) Wittr.

Pl. Scand. p. 15; Chætophoroideæ Harv. Man. p. 10; ex parte.

Gen. Chætophora Schrank.
Bair. Fl.

Chætophora pellucida Kjellm.
N. Ish. Algfl. p. 352.
Descr. Chætophora pellucida Kjellm. l. c.
   " " De-Toni, Syll. Alg. 1, p. 185.
Fig. " " Kjellm. l. c. t. 31, fig. 4—7.

I found this species in small number growing together with *Ulothrix flacca* on posts in the harbour of Vardö. The plant was not fully developed when collected at the end of July.

Distribution: Only found at Vardö, local and scarce.

Gen. Endoderma Lagerh.
Bidr. Sver. Algfl. p. 74.

Endoderma Wittrockii (Wille) Lagerh.
l. c.; Wille, Ny edoph. Alg. p. 3.
Descr. Entocladia Wittrockii Wille, l. c.
  Endoderma " De-Toni. Syll. Alg. 1, p. 209.
Fig. Entocladia " Wille, l. c. t. 1.
Exsicc. " " Wittr. et Nordst. Alg. exsicc. Nr. 408.

This species lives endophytic in *Pylaiella litoralis*, and perhaps also in other filiform algæ along the coast of East-Finmarken.

Distribution: Unknown to me. Found at Kiberg and Mehavn.

Gen. Bulbocoleon Pringsh.
Morph. Meeresalg. p. 8.

Bulbocoleon piliferum Pringsh.
l. c.
Descr. Bulbocoleon piliferum Pringsh. l. c.
        „   „   De-Toni, Syll. Alg. 1, p. 211.
Fig.   „   „   Pringsh. l. c. t. **1**.
Exsicc. „   „   Wittr. et Nordst. Alg. exsicc Nr. 407 et 911.

The species grows endophytic in *Halosaccion ramentaceum* and *Phloeospora tortilis* within the litoral zone.

Distribution: Found at Vardö and Berlevaag, but probably more commonly spread.

Fam. **Vaucheriaceæ** (Gray.) Dumort.
Comm. Bot. p. 71; Gray, Arrang. Brit. p. 288; lim. mut.

Gen. **Vaucheria** D. C.
in Vauch. Hist. des Conf. p. 25.

Vaucheria coronata Nordst.
in Bot. Not. 1879, p. 177.
Descr. Vaucheria coronata Nordst. l. c.
      „   „   De-Toni, Syll. Alg. 1, p. 403.
Fig.   „   „   Nordst. l. c. t. 1, fig. 1—9.

In the only place I met with this alga it occurred as a cushion-like cover on *Spongomorpha* and *Rhodochorton Rothii* a little above high-water mark, but in a very much exposed locality and, therefore, almost constantly washed over by the waves. The plant was provided with reproductive organs in the middle of August.

Distribution: Only found on the outer side of Hornö at Vardö, local and very scarce.

Fam. **Derbesiaceæ** Thur.
in Ann. d. Sc Nat. 3, 14, p. 231.

Gen. **Derbesia** Solier.
in Ann. d. Sc. Nat. 3, 7, p. 157.

Derbesia marina (Lyngb.) Solier
l. c. Vaucheria marina Lyngb. Hydr. Dan. p. 79.
Descr. Derbesia marina Solier l. c.
    „   „   De-Toni, Syll. Alg. 1, p. 426.
Fig.   „   „   Solier l. c. t. 9, fig. 1—17.
     Vaucheria   „   Lyngb. l. c. t. 22.
Exsicc. Derbesia   „   Wittr. et Nordst. Alg. exsicc. Nr. 952.

A sublitoral alga, which I found at the coast of East-Finmarken only attached to *Actinia* in about 5 fathoms water. At Vardö was brought to me a coral to which some specimens of this plant were fastened. It was said to have been picked up from a depth of about 40 fathoms. Specimens collected in the beginning of August were sterile.

Distribution: Found only at Kjelmö in Sydvaranger, scarce, and some few specimens brought to me at Vardö.

Fam. **Bryopsidaceæ** Thur.
in Le Jol. Liste Alg. Cherb. p. 14.

Gen. **Bryopsis** Lamour.
Ess. p. 281.

Bryopsis plumosa (Huds.) Ag.
Spec. Alg. 1, p. 448; Ulva plumosa Huds. Fl. Angl. p. 571.
Descr. Bryopsis plumosa Hauck, Meeresalg. p. 471.
Fig.   „   „   Harv. Phyc. Brit. t. 3.
Exsicc.   „   „   Aresch. Alg. Scand. exsicc. Nr. 422.

According to Philip Sewell, this species has been collected at Vardö. Cp. Sewell in Trans. and Proc. Bot. Soc. Edinburgh, 1889, p. 460.[1]

---
[1]. Philip Sewell, The Flora of the Coasts of Lapland and the

It seems doubtful to me whether the plant really occurs even in the eastern part of the district. G. W. Traill, who has determined Sewell's collection of algæ, has kindly communicated to me that, as the supposed *Bryopsis plumosa* was in very small fragments, and badly pressed on coarse botanical drying paper, he had some hesitation in identifying it.

Distribution: Unknown to me. It is said to have been found at Vardö.

Fam. **Characiaceæ** (Näg.) Wittr.
Gotl. och Öl Alg. p. 32; Näg. Gatt. einz. Alg. p. 64; excl. gen.

Gen. **Chlorochytrium** Cohn.
Biol. Pflanz. p. 102.

Chlorochytrium (?) inclusum Kjellm.
N. Ish. Algfl. p. 392.

Descr. Chlorochytrium (?) inclusum Kjellm. l. c.
        „   „   De-Toni, Syll. Alg. 1. p. 637.
Fig.   „   „   Kjellm. l. c. t. 31, fig. 8—17.

I found an endophytic alga in *Dumontia filiformis*, which I suppose belongs to this species. At Tromsö I have seen certain specimens in *Halosaccion ramentaceum*.

Distribution: Found at Mehavn, probably also occurring at other places.

Gen. **Codiolum** Al. Br.
Alg. unic. p. 19.

Yugor Straits (N.-W. Siberia), as observed during the Voyage of the „Labrador" in 1888; with Summarised List of all the Species known from the Islands of Novaya Zemlya and Waigatz, and from the North Coast of Western Siberia.

Codiolum cylindraceum Fosl.

in Tromsö Mus. Aarsh. X, p. 189; excl. f. minor.
Descr. Codiolum pusillum Fosl. Arkt. havalg. p. 12; excl. syn.
       „   cylindraceum Fosl. in Tromsö Mus. Aarsh. l. c.; excl. f. minor.
Fig.   „   pusillum Fosl. Arkt. havalg. t. 2, fig. 1.
Exsicc. „   „   Wittr. et Nordst. Alg. exsicc. **Nr.** 457.
    Syn. Codiolum pusillum Kjellm. N. Isb. Algfl. p. 389; ex parte.
          „   cylindraceum De-Toni, Syll. Alg. 1, p. 632; excl. f. minus.

Having had the opportunity of seeing Lyngbye's original specimen of his *Vaucheria (Codiolum) pusilla* from the Färöe Islands, I have shown, in Tromsö Mus. Aarsh. l. c., that the plant described by me in Arct. havalg. l. c. by the name of *Codiolum pusillum* is not identic with Lyngbye's plant, but ought to be regarded a separate species, taking *Codiolum* in the sense mentioned in Tromsö Mus. Aarsh. l. c. I therefore have called it *C. cylindraceum*.

In the eastern part of the district I met with this species in great number, growing on rocks near high-water mark, and almost fully agreeing with the form found some years ago at Gjesvær in West-Finmarken.

Distribution: Found at Pasvig, local but abundant.

Codiolum pusillum (Lyngb.) Fosl.

in Tromsö Mus. Aarsh, X, p. 190; Vaucheria pusilla Lyngb. Hydr. Dan. p. 79, t. 22 B.
Descr. Codiolum pusillum Fosl. l. c.
    Syn. Vaucheria pusilla De-Toni, Syll. Alg. 1, p. 408.
          Codiolum longipes Holmes, Alg. Brit. Nr. 33; sec. spec. ex herb. Holmes.
          „   pusillum Kjellm. N. Isb. Algfl. p. 389; ex parte.
          „   „   De-Toni, Syll. Alg. 1, p. 631; ex parte. Non Fosl. Arkt. havalg. p. 12.

This species is characterizing itself by its club generally being shorter than the stipe, subcylindric or not seldom elongated obovate. The stipe is very thin in the lower part, and is not always passing into the club without any limit. By Finmarkian specimens the club sometimes is somewhat thicker in proportion to the length than by specimens from the Färöe Islands, but otherwise coinciding with one another. The plant is smaller, and it has another general appearance than *C. cylindraceum*, the strata being thinner and the colour a little paler, and often it grows together with other smaller algæ, especially *Phycochromophyceæ*.

I have seen it growing almost side by side with the named species, on rocks in the upper part of the litoral zone.

Distribution: Found at Pasvig, pretty common and abundant.

Codiolum brevipes nob.

C. cylindraceum f. minor Fosl. in Tromsö Mus. Aarsh. l. c.

C. thallo 0.5—1 mm. longo; clava subcylindrica vel elongato-obovata, 350—700 μ longa; 35—80 μ crassa, stipitem longitudine superante. *Exsicc.* Codiolum cylindraceum f. minor Fosl. in Wittr. et Nordst. Alg. exsicc. Nr. 955.

Syn. Codiolum cylindraceum f. minus De-Toni, Syll. Alg. 1, p. 632.

In the above quoted paper I made a mistake in referring the present plant to *C. cylindraceum*. I thence only saw it in smaller number, and in some respects resembling *C. cylindraceum* I thought it ought to be referred to that species. Later I have found it in rather considerable abundance, and now it seems to me not to be referrible to the named species. It is, like theother species of the genus, rather variable, and perhaps most nearly related to *C. pusillum*, but the club is longer than the stipe and generally a little thicker, and often also with a rather distinct limit between the stipe and the club. On the other hand it resembles *C. Nordenskiöldianum* by the club being longer than the stipe and often elongated-obovate. But it seems to be a larger and coarser plant than that one. I am, therefore, obliged provisionally to regard it a distinct species.

The present plant grows on wood-work in the upper part of the litoral zone together with *Urospora penicilliformis*. Specimens collected in the beginning of August were sparingly zoosporiferous.

Distribution: Found at Vardö, pretty plentiful but local.

Codiolum intermedium Fosl.

in Tromsö Mus. Aarsh. X, p. 193.
Descr. Codiolum intermedium Fosl. l. c.'
Fig.   „   „   „   „ t. 2, fig. 1—12.
Exsicc. „   „   Wittr. et Nordst. Alg. exsicc. Nr. 954.

This species is more variable than any other of the genus. However it appears to be pretty well differentiated. The club is elongated-obovate, obovate or roundish, and the stipe often is rather sharply defined from the clava.

The plant grows on rocks and woodwork in the upper part of the litoral zone, together with other smaller algæ, as *Urospora*, *Calothrix* and *Glococapsa*. Specimens with zoospores have been taken in the earlier half of August.

Distribution: Found at Vardö, local and rather scarce, and at Kjelmö, scarce.

On the following page I give a comparative table of the species af *Codiolum* hitherto known.

	Total-Length.	The stipe. Length.	The stipe. Thickness.	The club. Length.	The club. Thickness.	
C. gregarium A. Br.	1000—1500 μ	600—1000 μ	22—29μ	250—500 μ	66—90μ	The club oblong, 1½—3 times shorter than the stipe.
C. cylindraceum Fosl.	1500—2700	600—1000	20—40	1000—1800	35—70	The club subcylindric, generally longer than the stipe, often 1½—3 times.
C. pusillum (Lyngb.) Fosl.	600—1300	400—800	20—30	200—600	40—75	The club subcylindric or elongated obovate, generally shorter than the stipe.
C. brevipes Fosl.	500—1000	150—400	18—30	350—700	35—80	The club subcylindric or elongated obovate, generally longer than the stipe.
C. longipes Fosl.	600—1200	350—650	30—65	250—500	70—120	The club elongated obovate, shorter than the stipe.
C. intermedium Fosl.	300—600	170—250	25—40	150—300	55—110	The club elongated obovate or roundish, mostly shorter than the stipe
C. Nordenskiöldianum Kjellm	175—400 (600)	60—190	10—16	100—250	25—50 (70)	The club mostly elongated obovate, longer than the stipe.

Gen. **Characium** Al. Br.
in Kütze. Spc. Alg. p. 203.

Characium marinum Kjellm.
N. Ish. Algfl. p. 388.

Descr. Characium sp. Kjellm. Spetsb. Thall. 2, p. 57.
„   marinum De-Toni, Syll. Alg. 1, p. 621.
Fig.   „   sp. Kjellm. l. c. t. 4, fig. 10.

I found some few specimens of this plant epiphytic on *Urospora penicilliformis* in the upper part of the litoral region. They are 30—42 µ long and 10—13 µ thick in the thickest part, bearing almost ripe zoospores in the later half of August.

Distribution: Only found at Vardö, rare.

Fam. **Palmellaceæ** (Dcsne.) Näg.
Gatt. einz. Alg. p. 61; Desne in Ann. d. Sc. Nat. II, 17, p.327; lim. mut.

Gen. Gloeocystis Näg.
Gatt. einz. Alg. p. 66.

Gloeocystis scopulorum Hansg.[1]
in lit.

„Vegetative Zellen ohne Hüllen 4 bis 6 µ, mit den Hullen 5 bis 8 µ breit, einzeln oder meist zu 2 bis 8 seltener mehrere familienweise vereinigt (8-zellige Familien sind etwa 20 µ breit), zu einem gelblichgrünem Gallertlager dicht zusammengehäuft. Gallerthülle deutlich geschichtet, farblos".

---

[1] Besides the species described by Prof. H a n s g i r g, he also has had the kindness to determine the following ones: Palmella mediterranea, Calothrix parasitica, Dichothrix gypsophila, Nodularia spumigena, Lyngbya luteo-fusca, jadertina, inundata, Oscillaria neapolitana, Pleurocapsa fuliginosa and Gloeocapsa crepidinum. Prof. Ch. F l a h a u l t has kindly determined Calothrix vivipara, parietina and some specimens of C. scopulorum.

This species «unterscheidet sich von der ihr am nächsten stehenden *Glococystis marina* Hansg. Oesterr. bot. Zeitschr. 1889, p. 42 hauptsächlich durch ihre Kleinheit«. It has been found in a sheltered locallity, growing on rocks at half-tide together with *Pleurococcus marinus*, washed over by a small freshwater-stream when the tide falls.

Distribution: Found at Kjelmö in Sydvaranger, local and rather scarce.

Gen. Urococcus Hass.
'Brit. Freshw. Alg. p. 322.

Urococcus Foslieanus Hansg.
in lit.

„Vegetative Zellen kugelig, seltener fast eiförmig, ohne Hüllen ɔ bis 18, mit diesen 15—25 µ breit, einzeln oder zu 2 bis 8 in kugeligen Familien vereinigt, mit chlorophüllgrünem Inhalte, in welchem später rothe Schleimtropfen (Hämatochrom) nicht selten in grösserer Menge auftreten, wodurch der Zellinhalt röthlich gefärbt erscheint. Zellhaut und die urococcusartig geschichtete, stielartige, aus mehreren oft 10 bis 15 Etagen aufgebaute Gallerthülle farblos". Tab. 3, fig. 4—6.

«Diese neue *Urococcus*-Art steht den auf feuchten Kalksteinfelsen vorkommenden *U. Hookerianus* Berk. et Hass. (*Hæmatococcus Hookerianus* Berk. et Hass. Brit. Freshw. Alg. p. 325, t. 80, fig. 4) am nächsten, unterscheidet sich aber wesentlich von ihr durch ihren nicht blutroth gefärbten Inhalt sowie den Standort». The plant occurs on rocks at high water mark jointly with *Calothrix scopulorum*, *Lyngbya* and other algæ, in exposed localities as well as sheltered ones.

Distribution: Found at Vardö, Bugönæs and Kjelmö, rather scarce. (It has also been found at Gratangen and Ryöen in Tromsö amt).

Gen. **Palmella** (Lyngb.) Näg.
<small>Gatt. einz. Alg. p. 66; Lyngb. Hydr. Dan. p. 203; char. mut.</small>

Palmella mediterranea Kütz.
<small>Phyc. gener. p. 271.</small>

Descr. Palmella mediterranea Kütz. Spec. Alg. p. 212.
       "   "   De Toni, Syll. Alg. 1, p. 682.
Fig.   "   "   Kütz. Tab. Phyc. 1, t. 14.

Litoral, growing on rocks in company with *Calothrix scopulorum*, *Lyngbya* and other algæ at high-water mark on somewhat exposed shore. At West-Finmarken it has been taken on woodwork (posts).

Distribution: Found in two different localities at Kjelmö in Sydvaranger, scarce, and at Sværholt, scarce. (Also found at Gjesvær in West-Finmarken, and at Tromsö).

Gen. **Dactylococcus** Näg.
<small>Gatt. einz. Alg. p. 85.</small>

Dactylococcus (?) litoralis Hansg.
in lit.

„Vegetative Zellen länglich eiförmig, 1 bis 1.5 μ breit, 2 bis 3 mal so lang, an beiden Enden abgerundet, mit gelblich oder olivengrünem Inhalte und dünner farbloser Membran, durch schief zu dem Längsdurchmesser der Mutterzelle liegende Scheidewände in zwei, seltener mehrere Tochterzellen sich theilend". Tab. 3, fig. 7.[1])

This species occurs at high-water mark together with *Lyngbya*, *Gloeocapsa* and other algæ.

Distribution: Found at Kjelmö, seems to be rare. (It has also been taken at Tromsö).

---

[1] „Da ich nicht constatiren könnte, ob die Tochterzellen auch in einen Schwärmenzustand übergehen können, wie bei *Dactylococcus infusionum* Näg., und da der Zellinhalt nicht rein chlorophüllgrün ist, so habe ich diese Alge oben als Dactylococcus (?) bezeichnet". Hansg. in lit.

Dactylococcus marinus Hansg.
in lit.

„Zellen meist sichelförmig, seltener fast spindelförmig, an beiden Enden allmälig verschmälert und in eine farblose Spitze auslaufend, in der Mitte 3 bis 3,5 μ breit, 10 bis 20 mal so lang, an der Spitze kaum 1 μ dick, beide Spitzen an den sichelförmig gekrümmten Exemplaren etwa 40 bis 60 μ von einander entfernt, mit gelbgrünem Inhalte (blos im mittleren Theile)". Tab. 3, fig. 8.

The species has been collected together with *Coilodesme bulligera* in rock-pools at half-tide.

Distribution: Only found at Kiberg, scarce.

Gen. Pleurococcus (Menegh.) Näg.
Gatt. einz. Alg. p. 64; Menegh. Nostoch. p. 38; char. mut.

Pleurococcus marinus Hansg.
in lit.

f. *typica*.

„Zellen kugelig, vor der Theilung elliptisch, meist 5 bis 10 μ breit (mit der Hülle) einzeln, einzeln oder zu 2 bis 4 zu 12 bis 20 μ breiten Familien vereinigt, mit chlorophüllgrünem Inhalte und bis 2 μ dicker, deutlich geschichteter Membran, unter anderen Algen zerstreut oder grössere Haufen bildend". Tab. 3, fig. 9.

f. *major* Hansg.
in lit.

„Zellen mit der Hülle 15 bis 20 μ breit (Zellumen meist 5 bis 10 μ breit), mit sehr (3 bis 5 μ] dicker, deutlich geschichteter farbloser Membran, sonst wie die typischen Form". Tab. 3, fig. 10.

This first known marine species of *Pleurococcus* occurs on rocks at high-water mark jointly with *Gloeocystis*, *Urospora* and other algæ, on open coasts as well as sheltered ones.

Distribution: Found at Vardö (f. *major*), Bugönæs, Kjelmö and Pasvig (f. *typica* and f. *major*), and it seems to be pretty common but mostly scarce. (It has also been taken at Tromsö and Gratangen in Tromsö amt).

Fam. Protococcaceæ (Menegh.)
Cenn. sul. org. p. 25; ex parte.

Gen. Protococcus (Ag.) Rabenh.
Fl. Eur. Alg. 3, p. 56; Ag. Syst. Alg. p. XVII; ex parte.

Protococcus marinus Kütz.
Phyc. gener. p. 169.
f. *Foslieana* Hansg.
in lit.

„Vegetative Zellen kugelig oder fast kugelig, mit der dünnen farblosen eng anliegenden Membran meist 10 bis 35 μ breit. Zellinhalt blutroth gefärbt, ölartig glänzend [blos an jungen Zellen ist der Inhalt chlorophüllgrün]". Tab. 3, fig. 11.

The species «unterscheidet sich von der typischen Form des *P. marinus* Kütz. hauptsächlich durch geringere Grösse und blutrothe (nicht braunlichrothe) Farbe des Zellinhaltes». It occurs on rocks at high-water mark in company with *Lyngbya*, *Gloeocapsa*, *Calothrix* and other algæ, in exposed as well as sheltered places.

Distribution: Found at Sværholt, Mehavn, Vardö, Bugönæs, Kjelmö and Pasvig, pretty common but mostly in small number. (Also found at Grindö, Tromsö, Ryöen, Vikran and Tovig in Tromsö amt).

Protococcus ovalis Hansg.
in lit.

„Lager gelblichgrün, formlos, wenig schleimig. Vegetative Zellen eiförmig oder elliptisch, seltener fast rundlich, meist 8 bis 10 μ breit, 9 bis 12 μ lang, dünnhäutig mit gelbgrünem oft ölartig glänzendem Inhalte, einzeln oder gehäuft". Tab. 3, fig. 12.

This species grows on rocks at high-water mark together with other smaller algæ.

Distribution: Found at Vardö, scarce, and at Sværholt, rare.

Ser. Schizophyceæ Cohn.
in Jahresber. Schles. Ges. 1879, p. 279.

Subser. I. Phycochromophyceæ Rabenh.
Fl. Eur. Alg. 1, p. 1.

Fam. Rivulariaceæ (Harv.) Born. et Flah.
Rev. Nost. 1, p. 338; Harv. in Hook. Brit. Fl. 5, p. 262; lim. mut.

Subfam. I. Leptochæteæ Born. et Flah.
Rev. Nost. 1, p. 340.

Gen. Leptochæte Borzi.
in N. Giorn. bot. ital. 14, p. 298.

Leptochæte marina Hansg.
in lit.

„Lager hautartig, dünn, braungelb bis schwärzlich braun. Fäden dicht gehäuft, seltener vereinzelt, am unteren dickeren Ende mit der Scheide meist 1.5 bis 2, seltner 3 bis 5 μ, am oberen 0.7 oder 0.5, seltener bis 1 μ breit, an der Spitze abgerundet, deutlich gegliedert, oft nur 20 bis 60 μ lang, mehr oder weniger gekrümmt. Veget. Zellen $1/2$ bis $3/4$, seltener bis 1 mal so lang als breit, mit fein gekörntem, fast homogenem, blass blaugrünem oder olivengelblichem Inhalte, an den Scheidenwänden nicht oder unmerklich eingeschnürt. Endzellen abgerundet, nicht in farblose Haarspitze auslaufend. Scheiden meist eng anliegend, nicht deutlich geschichtet, am unteren, dickeren Fadenende goldgelb bis bräunlichgelb, am oberen, verdünnten, fast farblosen Theile meist hyalin und allmälig verschwindend".

The species occurs on rocks mostly at high-water mark in company with *Calothrix* and other smaller algæ. It appears in exposed as well as sheltered places.

Distribution: Found at Sværholt, Vardö (Hornö) and at Bugönæs in Sydvaranger, local and rather scarce. (It has also been found at Tromsö, Ryöen and Vikran in Tromsö amt).

Subfam. II. **Mastichotricheæ** Kütz.
Phyc. gener. p. 231.

Gen. **Calothrix** (Ag.) Thur.
Nostoch. p. 5; Ag. Syst. Alg. p. XXIV; char. mut.

Calothrix confervicola (Roth.) Ag.
Syst. Alg. p. 70; Conferva confervicola Roth, Cat. Bot. 3, p. 192.
Descr. Calothrix confervicola Born. et Flah. Rev. Nost. 1. p. 349.
Fig.   „   „   Born. et Thur. Not. Alg. 1, t. 3.
   „   „   Harv. Phyc. Brit. t. 254.
Exsicc.   „   „   Wyatt, Alg. Danm. Nr. 229.
   „   „   Aresch. Alg. Scand. exsicc. Ser. 1, Nr. 49.
Leibleinia confervicola Aresch. Alg. Scand. exsicc. Nr. 192.
Syn. Oscillaria confervicola Lyngb. Hydr. Dan. p. 94.
   „   zostericola Lyngb. l. c.
Leibleinia zostericola Aresch. Phyc. Scand. p. 439.
   „   confervicola Aresch. l. c. p. 440.

This species has been found epiphytic on *Phlocospora tortilis* and *Ectocarpus*, in sheltered localities.

Distribution: Found at Kirkenæs and Bugönæs in Sydvaranger, rare.

Calothrix scopulorum (Web. et Mohr) Ag.
Syst. Alg. p. 70; Conferva scopulorum Web. et Mohr, Reise p. 193.
Descr. Calothrix scopulorum Born. et Flah. Rev. Nost. 1, p. 353.
Fig.   „   „   Born. et Thur. Not. Alg. 2, t. 38.
   „   „   Harv. Phyc. Brit. t. 58. B.

Exsicc. Calothrix scopulorum Aresch. Alg. Scand. exsicc. Nr. 235.
   „   „   Wittr. et Nordst. Alg. exsicc. Nr. 484 et 852.
   Mastigonema velutinum Wolle in Wittr. et Nordst. l. c. Nr. 388.
Syn. Oscillaria scopulorum Lyngb. Hydr. Dan. p. 93.
   Calothrix   „   Aresch. Phyc. Scand. p. 438; ex parte.

Litoral, occurring on rocks and stones at high-water mark, often spreading widely over the rocks in great masses, mostly on open coast together with other smaller algæ. Once I met with it in the lower part of the zone, at Bugönæs in Sydvaranger.

Distribution: Common and abundant in most places especially along the open part ot the coast, for inst. Sværholt, Vardö, Bugönæs, Kjelmö and Pasvig.

Calothrix parasitica (Chauv.) Thur.
   Nostoch. p. 381; Rivularia parasitica Chauv. Rech. p. 41.
Descr. Calothrix parasitica Born. et Flah. Rev. Nost. 1, p. 357.
Fig.   „   „   Born. et Thur. Not. Alg. 2, t. 27, fig. 7—10.
Exsicc. „   „   Wittr. et Nordst. Alg. exsicc. Nr. 854.
   Schizosiphon parasiticum Le Jol. Alg. mar. Cherb. Nr. 237.

This species appears scattered in the layer of *Hypheothrix litoralis*, the latter together with *Calothrix scopulorum* and other algæ, on exposed rocks at high-water mark.

Distribution: Only found at Kjelmö in Sydvaranger, seems to be rare.

Calothrix vivipara Harv.
   Ner. Bor. Am. 3, p. 106.
Descr. Calothrix vivipara Born. et Flah. Rev. Nost. 1, p. 362.

The species lives on rocks or in shallow rock-pools at high-water mark, on exposed places.

Distribution: Only found on a small island in the neighbourhood of Kjelmö in Sydvaranger, local but pretty plentiful.

Calothrix parietina (Näg.) Thur.
Nostoch. p. 381; Schizosiphon parietinus Näg. in Kütz. Spec. Alg.
p. 327.

Descr. Calothrix parietina Born. et Flah. Rev. Nost. 1, p. 366.
Fig. Mastichonema caespitosum Kütz. Tab. Phyc. 2, t. 16.
Schizosiphon salinus Kütz. l. c. t. 47.
„ decoloratus Kütz. l. c.
Exsicc. Calothrix parietina Wittr. et Nordst. Alg. exsicc. Nr. 659 et 751.

This species occurs scattered among other smaller algæ on exposed rocks at high-water mark.

Distribution: Only found at Kjelmö in Sydvaranger, scarce.

Gen. Dichothrix Zanard.
Enum. p. 89.

Dichothrix gypsophila (Kütz.) Born. et Flah.
Rev. Nost. 1, p. 377; Schizosiphon gypsophilus Kütz. Phyc. gener.
p. 234.

Descr. Dichothrix gypsophila Born. et Flah. l. c.
Fig. Schizosiphon Kützingianus Kütz. Tab. Phyc. 2, t. 50,
„ cinctus Kütz. l. c. t. 51.
„ gypsophilus Kütz. l. c.
Exsicc. Dichothrix gypsophila Wittr. et Nordst. Alg. exsicc. Nr. 859.

In the only place where I met with this species it grew on smaller stones in a shallow and somewhat muddy and sheltered lagoon at high-water mark, partly dry and partly submersed, forming somewhat gelatinous, rough layers of a dark yellow-brown colour.

Distribution: Only found at Bugönæs (Bugö) in Sydvaranger, local but abundant.

Fam. **Nostocaceæ** (Kütz.) Thur.
Nostoch. p. 6; Kütz. Phyc. gener. p. 203; lim mut.

ubfam. **Anabæneæ** Born. et Flah.
Rev. Nost. 4, p. 180.

Gen. Nostoc Vauch.
Hist. cl. Conf. p. 203.

Nostoc maculiforme Born. et Flah.
Rev. Nost. 4, p. 189.

f. *norvegica* Hansg.
in lit.

"Fäden meist 3 bis 4, junge auch 2.5 μ dick, ohne deutliche Gallertscheiden. Veget. Zellen mit hell blaugrünem Inhalte, 1 bis 2 mal seltener blos $1/2$ mal so lang als breit, Heterocysten fast kugelig oder elliptisch etwa 5 μ breit; sonst wie die typische Form".

The form has been found in a sheltered lagoon at high-water mark together with other algæ, as *Cladophora*, *Ectocarpus* and *Nodularia spumigena*.

Distribution: Only found at Bugönæs in Sydvaranger, local and scarce.

Gen. Nodularia Mert.
in Jürg. Alg. aqu. 15, Nr. 4.

Nodularia spumigena Mert.
l. c.

f. *litorea* (Kütz.) Born. et Flah.
Rev. Nost. 4, p. 246; Spermosira litorea Kütz. Phyc. gener. p. 213.
Descr. Nodularia spumigena β litorea Born. et Flah. l. c.
Fig.   „   litorea Born. et Thur. Not. Alg. 2, t. 29.
Spermosira litorea Harv. Phyc. Brit. t. 113, C.

The above quoted form of this species was found together with the preceding one in a lagoon at high-water mark.

Distribution: Found only at Bugönæs in Sydvaranger, local and scarce.

Fam. Oscillariaceæ (Ag.) Wittr.

Pl. Scand. p. 53; Oscillatorineæ Ag. Syst. Alg. p. XXIV; lim. mut.

Gen. Lyngbya (Ag.) Thur.
Nostoch. p. 4; Ag. Syst. Alg. p. XXV; char. emend.

Lyngbya luteo-fusca (Ag.) J. G. Ag.
Alg. med. p. 11; Calothrix luteo-fusca Ag. Aufz. Nr. 41.
Descr. Lyngbya luteo-fusca Hauck, Meeresalg. p. 505.
      "   "   Farl. New. Engl. Alg. p. 35.
Fig.   "   "   Kütz. Tab. Phyc. 1, t. 88.
Exsicc.   "   "   Wittr. et Nordst. Alg. exsicc. Nr. 280.

This species occurs on rocks at high-water mark jointly with *Calothrix scopulorum* and other algæ. I have only met with it in exposed places.

Distribution: Found at Kjelmö in Sydvaranger and at Vardö, scattered and very scarce. (It has also been found at Tromsö).

Lyngbya semiplena (Ag.) J. G. Ag.
Alg. Med. p. 11; Calothrix semiplena Ag. Aufz. Nr. 40.
Descr. Lyngbya semiplena Hauck, Meeresalg. p. 505.
Fig. Leibleinia Meneghiniana Kütz. Tab. Phyc. 1, t. 84.

I found this plant in a much exposed locality, forming membraneously, often somewhat thick and smooth strata on rocks, or in the margin of rock-pools at high-water mark, and a little higher up.

Distribution: Found at Vardö (Hornö), local and rather scarce. (The plant has also been collected at West-Finmarken and at Tromsö).

Lyngbya jadertina (Menegh.) Hansg.
in Oesterr. bot. Zeitschr. 1889, p. 42; Oscillaria jadertina Menegh. sec. Rabenh. Fl. Eur. Alg. 2, p. 89.
Descr. Leptothrix jadertina Kütz. Spec. Alg. p. 265.
Fig.   "   "   "   Tab. Phyc. 1, t. 65.

Syn. Leptothrix marina Kütz. Phyc. germ. p. 165
Hypheothrix jadertina Rabenh. Fl. Eur. Alg. 2, p. 89.

Litoral, appearing together with *Calothrix* and other algæ on rocks at high-water mark, or sometimes in the lower part of the zone.

Distribution: Found at Sværholt, Mehavn, Vardö, Kiberg, Bugönæs, Kjelmö and Pasvig, at most places common and rather plentiful. (The plant has also been found at Tromsö, Ryöen, Gratangen and Tovig in Tromsö amt).

Lyngbya inundata (Kütz.) Hansg.
in Wittr. et Nordst. Alg. exsicc. Nr. 776: Phormidium inundatum Kütz. Phyc. gener. p. 193.
Descr. Phormidium inundatum Kütz. Spec. Alg. p. 251.
Fig. „ „ „ Tab. Phyc. 1, t. 45.
Exsicc. Lyngbya (Phormidium) inundata Wittr. et Nordst. Alg. exsicc. Nr. 776.

I met with this species at a single place only. It grew in a small and shallow rock-pool (or chiefly in the margin of the pool) at or perhaps a little above high-water mark in a rather exposed locality, and jointly with *Calothrix scopulorum*. The Finmarkian specimens belong to the form *adultior*. Cp. Wittr. et Nordst. l. c.

Distribution: Found at Vardö, local and very scarce. (It has also been taken at Tromsö).

Gen. **Hypheothrix** Kütz.
Phyc. gener. p. 229; Spec. Alg. p. 266.

Hypheothrix litoralis Hansg.
in lit. (Lyngbya (Hypheothrix) litoralis Hansg.)

"Lager schmutzig blaugrün, dünnhäutig, mehr oder weniger schleimig. Fäden 0.5 bis 1.5 μ breit (mit den Scheiden), meist gekrümmt und leicht unter einander verflochen, mit dünnen eng anliegenden, farblosen Scheiden. Zellen 1 bis $1^1/_2$ mal so lang als breit, mit hell blaugrünem Inhalte".

«Diese der *Lyngbya jadertina* am nächsten stehende Art unterscheidet sich durch die sehr zarten Fäden von allen bisher beschriebenen marinen *Lyngbya*-Arten aus der Section *Hypheothrix*«. The species grows on rocks at high-water mark in company with *Calothrix*, *Codiolum* and other algæ

Distribution: Found at Vardö, Kjelmö, Pasvig and Bugönæs, scarce. (It has also been found at Tromsö, Ryöen and Gratangen in Tromsö amt).

Gen. **Oscillaria** (Bosc.) Thur.
Nostoch. p. 4; Bosc. sec. Thur. l. c.

Oscillaria neapolitana Kütz.
Phyc. gener. p. 185.
Descr. Oscillaria neapolitana Hauck, Meeresalg. p. 509.
Fig. „ „ Kutz Tab. Phyc. 1, t. 39.

The species has been found in a lagoon at high-water mark jointly with *Nostoc*, *Nodularia* and *Polycystis*.

Distribution: Found at Bugönæs in Sydvaranger, local and scarce. (It has also been collected at Tromsö).

Gen. **Spirulina** Turp.
sec. Thur. Nostoch. p. 7.

Spirulina tenuissima Kütz.
Phyc. gener. p. 183.
Descr. Spirulina tenuissima Farl. New Engl. Alg. p 31.
„ „ Hauck, Meeresalg. p. 511.
Fig. „ „ Kütz. Tab. Phyc. 1, t. 37.
„ „ Farl. l. c. t. 1, fig. 4.
„ „ Harv. Phyc. Brit. t. 105, C.
Exsicc. „ „ Wittr. et Nordst. Alg. exsicc. Nr. 395.

The species occurs on rocks in the upper part of the litoral zone together with other smaller algæ, or found in rock-pools at half tide together with *Coilodesme bulligera*, or epiphytic on *Vaucheria coronata* a little above high-water mark. It is here 2.8 µ thick.

Distribution: Found at Vardö, local and scarce, at Kiberg, and at Bugönæs and Kjelmö in Sydvaranger, rare.

Fam. **Chamæsiphonaceæ** Borzi.
in Giorn. bot. ital. 10, p. 256.

Gen. **Chamæsiphon** A. Br. et Grün.
in Rabenh. Fl. Eur. Alg. 2, p. 148.

Chamæsiphon marinus Wille
in Dijmphna-Togt. zool. bot. Udb. p. 4.
Descr. Chamæsiphon marinus Wille l. c.
Fig. „ „ „ „ t. 13, fig. 1.

I have referred to this species a small *Chamæsiphon* nearly 1 µ thick, growing on *Spongomorpha intermedia* and *Ulothrix flacca*.

Distribution: Found at Vardö and Kiberg, rare.

Fam. **Chroococcaceæ** (Näg.) Wittr.
Pl. Scand. p. 56; Näg. Gatt. einz. Alg. p. 44; lim. mut.

Gen. **Pleurocapsa** Thur.
in Hauck, Meeresalg. p. 515.

Pleurocapsa fuliginosa Hauck.
Meeresalg. p. 515.
Descr. Pleurocapsa fuliginosa Hauck. l. c.
Fig. „ „ „ „ fig. 231.

Litoral, occurring on rocks at high-water mark jointly with other smaller algæ.

Distribution: Found at Kjelmö in Sydvaranger, rare.

(It has also been found at Tromsö, Ryöen and Gratangen in Tromsö amt).

Gen. Polycystis Kütz.
Tab. Phyc. 1, p. 7.

Polycystis litoralis Hansg.
in lit.

„Familien kugelig, elliptisch oder von unregelmässiger Form, meist mehrere neben einander, oft zusammenfliessend, mit ziemlich dicker, farbloser, gemeinsamer Gallerthülle bis 210 μ im Durchmesser, kleinere Familien oft nur 30 bis 60 μ breit, 1 bis 2 mal so lang. Vegetative Zellen rundlich oder elliptisch, 3 bis 4 seltener bis 5 μ breit, 1 bis 2 mal so lang, mit dünner farbloser Membran und hell blaugrünem Inhalte, oft dicht gehäuft". Tab. 3, fig. 13.

The plant has been collected in a lagoon at high-water mark in company with *Cladophora*, *Ectocarpus*, *Nodularia*, *Nostoc* and *Oscillaria*.

Distribution: Only found at Bugönæs in Sydvaranger, local and scarce.

Gen. Aphanocapsa Näg.
Gatt. einz. Alg. p. 52.

Aphanocapsa marina Hansg.
in lit.

„Lager formlos, gallertig, von schmutzig spangrüner, trocken fast schwärzlichgrüner Farbe, ziemlich weit ausgebreitet. Vegetative Zellen rundlich 0.4 bis 0.5 μ breit, fast ebenso lang, mit blass blaugrünem Inhalte und dünner farbloser Membran, einzeln oder zu zwei neben einander in gemeinsamer farbloser Gallerte eingebettet".

The species has been found in a rock-pool at or a little above high-water mark in company with *Lyngbya* and other smaller algæ.

Distribution: Only found at Pasvig in Sydvaranger, local and scarce

Gen. Gloeocapsa (Kütz.) Näg.
Gatt. einz. Alg. p. 47; Kütz. Phyc. gener. p. 173; char mut.

Gloeocapsa crepidinum Thur.
Born. et Thur. Not. Alg. 1, p. 1; Protococcus crepidinum Thur. in Mem. Soc. Sc. nat. d. Cherb, 2, p. 388.
Descr. Gloeocapsa crepidinum Farl. New Engl. Alg. p. 27.
           "   "   Hauck, Meeresalg. p. 513.
Fig.   "   "   Born. et Thur. Not. Alg. 1, t. 1, fig. 1—3.
Exsicc. Protococcus "   Le Jol. Alg. mar. Cherb. Nr. 16.
    Syn. Pleurococcus crepidinum Rabenh. Fl. Eur. Alg. 3, p. 25.

This species lives on rocks or in small pools at or a little above high-water mark, mostly together with other algæ, on open coasts as well as sheltered ones.

Distribution: Found at Sværholt, Vardö, Bugönæs, Kjelmö and Pasvig, pretty common but not plentiful. (The plant has also been collected at Tromsö, Ryöen, Vikran, Gratangen and Grindö in Tromsö amt).

Gen. Entophysalis Kütz.
Phyc. gener. p. 177.

Entophysalis granulosa Kütz.
l. c.
Descr. Entophysalis granulosa Hauck, Meeresalg. p. 513.
Fig.   "   "   Born. et Thur. Not. Alg. 1, t. 1, fig 4—5.
       "   "   Kütz. Tab. Phyc. 1, t. 32.
Exsicc. "   "   Wittr. et Nordst. Alg. exsicc. Nr. 294.

I have met with this species on rocks near high-water mark scattered among *Calothrix scopulorum* and other marine algæ, in exposed places, and also somewhat above tide mark, on stones in a small grot at the inner end of a deep bay,

Distribution: Found at Kjelmö in Sydvaranger, rare, and in Trifanshulen in the neighbourhood of Elvenæs in Sydvaranger, scarce.

Subser. II. Schizomycetes Cohn.
Beitr. z. Biol. d. Pflanz.

Fam. Coccaceæ Zopf.
Spaltpilze p. 46.

Gen. Leptothrix Kütz.
Phyc. gener. p. 197.

Leptothrix subtilissima Hansg.
in lit.

„Fäden mit einem Ende festsitzend, sehr dünn, etwa 0.3 µ dick, meist nur 1 bis 2 µ lang, seltener länger mit undeutlicher Gliederung, farblos, gerade oder leicht gekrümmt, frei aufrecht oder an der Oberfläche anderer Meeresalgen liegend, einzeln oder gehäuft".

The species occurs on *Ectocorpus*, *Cladophora*, *Lyngbya* and other algæ within the litoral zone.

Distribution: Found at Vardö, Kiberg and Bugönæs, scarce.

Leptothrix arctica nob.

L. adnata, solitaria vel subpenicillata, flexuoso-curvata, dilute viridis, apicem versus poullo attenuata, circ. 300—800 µ longa, 2.5—4 µ crassa, cellulis duplo brevioribus.

The species much resembles *Leptothrix rigidula* Kütz. Tab. Phyc. 1, t. 59 in habit, but it is a coarser plant, and the cells are shorter than by that species, their length is generally half the diameter. The plant is litoral as well as sublitoral. In the former case I met with it on several larger algæ, as *Cladophora glaucescens*, *Isthmoplea*, *Ptilota pec-*

tinata and *Pt. elegans*. In the latter case it has been found on *Ptilota plumosa* on a depth of 2—5 fathoms. It has only been found in exposed places.

Distribution: Probably commonly spread along the whole coast and at some places rather plentiful, for inst. Kjöllefjord and Vardö. I have seen it at Sværholt, Kjöllefjord, Omgang, Berlevaag, Vardö, Kiberg and Kjelmö.

Gen. Micrococcus Cohn.
Beitr. z. Biol. d. Pflanz. I, p. 151.

Micrococcus sordidus Schröt.
sec. Hansg. in lit.

f. *marina* Hansg.
in lit.

„Vegetative Zellen fast kugelig, kaum 1 μ breit, farblos, locker zu einem gallertigen, fast farblosem Lager vereinigt".

This plant appears on rocks in the upper part of the litoral zone together with other smaller algæ.

Distribution: Found at Vardö, rather scarce. (It has also been collected at Tromsö).

Gen. Sarcina Goods.
in Ann. and Magaz. of N. Hist. 19, p. 334.

Sarcina litoralis (Oerst.) Pouls.
Mikr. Planteorg. p. 26; Erythroconis litoralis Oerst. Beretn. p. 555. Merismopedia litoralis Warm. Pact. p. 351; Rabenh. Fl. Eur. Alg. 2, p. 57.

? f. *norvegica* Hansg.
in lit.

„Zellen fast kugelig, vor der Theilung elliptisch, 0.5 bis 1 μ breit, mit fast farblosem oder blass rosenroth gefärbtem Inhalte, zu rundlichen oder knollenförmigen, 10 bis 20 μ breiten und langen (die nicht kugelrunden oft bis 30 µ langen) Familien vereinigt, welche nicht selten gelappt sind". Tab. 3, fig. 14.

The species occurs on rocks at high-water mark in company with *Lyngbya jadertina* and other smaller algæ, in exposed as well as sheltered localities.

Distribution: Found at Sværholt, Mehavn, Vardö, Kiberg, Bugönæs, Kjelmö and Pasvig, pretty common but scarce. (It has also been found at Tromsö, Ryöen and Gratangen in Tromsö amt).

Errata.

Pag. 102, *Gobia baltica*: *Exsicc.* and *Syn. Dictyosiphon (Coilonema) Chordaria* var. A r e s c h. to strike; and to add: The plant is 3—5 cm. long, proportionally thinner than the habit-figure by G o b i l. c. and in habit somewhat reminding of *Physematoplea attenuata*.

Explanation of the Plates.

Plate 1.

Halosaccion pubescens.

Habit-figure. $1/2$.

Plate 2.

Halosaccion pubescens.

Fig. 1. Part of a transverse section of the lower part of the frond. $320/1$.

Bangia virescens.

Fig. 2—6. Vegetative threads. $230/1$.
« 7—9. Sporocarps and antheridia (?). $230/1$.

Enteromorpha microphylla.

Fig. 10. Part of the base of the frond, about 3 mm. from the callus, seen from the surface. $230/1$.
« 11. Transverse section of the same part. $230/1$.
« 12. Part of the frond towards the middle, seen from the surface. $230/1$.
« 13. Part of the upper and zoospore-bearing part of the frond, seen from the surface. $230/1$.
« 14. Transverse section of the same part. $230/1$.
« 15—16. Part of a transverse section of the middle of two different specimens. $230/1$.

Pilinia minor.

Fig. 17—22. Young and elder specimens of the plant. $600/1$.

Plate 3.

Ulothrix flacca.

Fig. 1. Part of a vegetative thread with very short cells in longitudinal direction of the frond. $^{230}/_1$.

« 2—3. Parts of a zoospore-bearing thread. $^{230}/_1$.

Urococcus Foslicanus.

Fig. 4—5. Two cells with annulated, gelatinous stalk. $^{600}/_1$.

« 6. A cell which has divided itself into two daughter-cells; *h.* small drops of Hämatochrom. $^{600}/_1$.

Dactylococcus (?) litoralis.

Fig. 7. A vegetative cell before, during and after the division. $^{900}/_1$.

Dactylococcus marinus.

Fig. 8. Vegetative cells of the plant. $^{600}/_1$.

Pleurococcus marinus f. typica.

Fig. 9. A young cell, then a three- and a four-celled family. $^{600}/_1$.

Pleurococcus marinus f. major.

Fig. 10. A vegetative cell of the plant. $^{600}/_1$.

Protococcus marinus f. Foslicana.

Fig. 11. A vegetative cell of the plant. $^{600}/_1$.

Protococcus ovalis.

Fig. 12. Vegetative cells of the plant. $^{600}/_1$.

Polycystis litoralis.

Fig. 13. Two families of the plant. $^{600}/_1$.

Sarcina litoralis (?) f. norvegica.

Fig. 14. A tuberous family of the plant. $^{600}/_1$.

REGISTER.

Actinococcus Kütz.	55
roseus [Suhr.] Kütz.	55
Ahnfeltia [Fr.] J. G. Ag.	32
plicata [Huds.] Fr.	32
Alaria Grev.	71
esculenta [L.] Grev.	71
f. pinnata [Gunn.] Fosl.	71
grandifolia J. G. Ag.	73
linearis Strömf.	74
membranacea J. G. Ag.	72
musæfolia J. G. Ag.	71
Pylaii [De la Pyl.] J. G. Ag.	71
Anabænæ Born. et Flah.	164
Antithamnion [Näg.] Thur.	45
boreale Gobi [Kjellm.]	47
f. typica Kjellm.	47
f. corallina Rupr. (Kjellm.)	47
floccosum [Müll.] Kleen	45
f. atlantica J. G. Ag.	45
plumula var. boreale Gobi	47
Pylaisæi [Mont.] Farl.	46
f. typica	46
f. norvegica Kjellm.	46
Aphanocapsa Näg.	169
marina Hansg.	169
Ascophyllum nodosum Gobi	64
Asperococcaceæ Farl.	88
Asperococcus Lamour.	88
echinatus [Mert.] Grev.	88
Bangia [Lyngb.] Kütz.	61
crispa Lyngb.	61
fuscopurpurea (Dillw.) Lyngb.	61

Bangia virescens Fosl.	62
Blastosporaceæ Jess.	126
Bryopsidaceæ Thur.	149
Bryopsis Lamour.	149
plumosa [Huds.] Ag.	149
Bulbocoleon Pringsh.	147
piliferum Pringsh.	148
Calliblepharis ciliata Kleen	25
Callithamnion [Lyngb.] Thur.	44
corallina Rupr.	47
Daviesii auct.	51
β *secundatum* Lyngb.	53
efflorescens J. G. Ag.	50
floridulum auct.	49
mesocarpum auct.	50
microscopicum Näg.	54
Pylaisæi auct.	46
roseum β *tenue* Lyngb.	44
Rothii auct.	48
scopulorum Ag.	44
secundatum auct.	53
sparsum auct.	49
virgatulum auct.	51
Calothrix (Ag.) Thur.	161
confervicola [Roth.] Ag.	161
parasitica (Chauv.) Thur.	162
parietina (Näg.) Thur.	163
scopulorum [W. & M.] Ag.	161
vivipara Harv.	162
Capsicarpella sphærophora auct.	109
Castagnea virescens auct.	90
Zosteræ Kleen	90

Ceramiaceæ [Ag] Hauck.	38	*Chondrus crisp. ε pumilus* Lgb.	25
Ceramium [Lyngb.] Harv.	38	Chorda [Stackh.] Lamour	86
botryocarpum Harv.	39	filum [L.] Stackh.	86
rubrum (Huds.) Ag.	39	var. *fistulosa* auct.	96
f. decurrens J. G. Ag.	39	f. subtomentosa Aresch.	86
f. genuina	39	f. typica	86
f. pedicellata Duby	39	*lomentaria* auct.	96
f. prolifera J. G. Ag.	39	var. *antumnalis* Aresch.	96
secundatum Lyngb.	39	tomentosa Lyngb.	87
strictum Grev. et Harv.	38	f. subfulva Fosl.	87
Chætomorpha Kütz.	141	f. typica	87
melagonium [W. & M.] Ktz.	141	Chordaceæ (Kütz.) Rke.	86
f. rupincola Aresch.	141	Chordaria [Ag.] J. G. Ag.	89
f. typica	141	*attenuata* Fosl.	97
tortuosa [Dillw.] Kütz.	142	flagelliformis [Müll.] Ag.	8.
Chætophora Schrank.	147	Chordariaceæ (Ag.) Rke.	
marina Lyngb.	91	Chroococcaceæ [Näg] Wittr.	1
pellucida Kjellm.	147	Chroolepediaceæ [Rabenh.] Bzi.	146
Chætophoraceæ (Harv.) Wittr.	147	Chytridium plumulæ Cohn	48
Chætopteris Kütz	106	Cladophora Kütz.	135
plumosa [Lyngb.] Kütz.	106	*fracta* Kleen	140
Chamæsiphon A. Br. et Grün.	168	glaucescens [Griff.] Harv.	136
marinus Wille	168	*glaucescens* Fosl.	136, 137
Chamæsiphonaceæ Borzi.	168	gracilis [Griff.] Harv.	13"
Chantransia [D. C.] Fr.	50	f. borealis Fosl.	137
Daviesii [Dillw.] Thur.	51	*hirta* var. *borealis* F. sl.	1:6
efflorescens [J. Ag.] Kjellm.	50	Hutchinsiæ [Dillw] Kütz	
f. tenuis Kjellm.	51	f. distans [Kütz.]	136
microscopica (Näg.) Fosl.	54	*lanosa* auct.	133
secundata [Lyngb.] Thur.	53	rupestris [L.] Kütz.	135
virgatula [Harv.] Thur.	51	f. submarina Fosl.	135
f. *Farlowii* Kjellm.	51	f. typica	135
Characiaceæ [Näg.] Wittr.	150	*sericea* Kleen	136
Characium Al. Br.	155	*uncialis* auct.	134
marinum Kjellm.	155	Cladophoraceæ (Hass.) Wittr.	129
Chlorochytrium Cohn	150	*Cladosiphon balticus* Gobi	102
inclusum Kjellm.	150	Coccaceæ Zopf.	171
Chlorophyceæ [Rabenh.] Wittr.	113	Codiolum Al. Br.	150
Chondrus [Stackh.] J. G. Ag.	83	brevipes Fosl.	152
crispus (L.) Lyngb.	33	cylindraceum Fosl.	151

Codiolum cylindr. minor Fosl.	152
intermedium Fosl.	153
longipes Holmes	151
pusillum [Lyngb.] Fosl.	151
pusillum auct.	151
Coilodesme Strömf.	94
bulligera Strömf.	94
Coilodesmeæ Fosl.	94
Coilonema Aresch.	102
chordaria Aresch.	102
f. bahusiensis Aresch.	102
Ekmani Aresch.	102
filiformis Fosl.	103
Finmarkicum Fosl.	103
Conferva arcta auct.	131
atropurpurea Wg.	61
atrorubens Wg.	20
centralis Lyngb.	131
diaphana Wg.	39
dichotoma Gunn.	90
elongata Gunn.	90
flaccida Lyngb.	93
glomerata marina Wg.	136
hormoides Aresch.	145
litoralis Wg.	110, 112
litoralis Gunn.	39
melagonium auct.	141
mirabilis Aresch.	145
obtusangula auct.	139
omissa Gunn.	18
pannosa Aresch.	139
pennata Wg.	107, 108
polymorpha auct.	18
rupestris auct.	135
rupestris Gunn.	39
seposita Gunn.	39
siliculosa Sommerf.	110
speciosa auct.	145
squarrosa Gunn.	14
stricta Wg.	16
Conferva tortuosa Aresch.	142
uncialis auct.	133
Confervaceæ (Bonn.) Lagerh.	145
Corallina (Tourn.) Lamour.	5
officinalis L.	5
f. flexilis Kjellm.	5
f. robusta Kjellm.	5
f. typica	5
Corallinaceæ (Lamour.) Hauck.	5
Cruoria Middendorffi [Rupr.] Kjellm.	55
pellita Rupr.	55
Cystoclonium Kütz.	30
purpurasc.us [Huds.] Ktz.	30
Dactylococcus Näg.	157
litoralis Hansg.	157
marinus Hansg.	158
Delesseria (Lamour.) J. G. Ag.	21
alata (Huds.) Lamour.	21
var. *angustissima* Kleen	21
sanguinea auct.	24
sinuosa (G. et W.) Lamour.	22
f. lingulata Ag.	23
f. quercifolia Turn.	22
f. typica	22
Delesseriaceæ J. G. Ag.	21
Derbesia Sol.	149
marina (Lyngb.) Sol.	149
Derbesiaceæ Thur.	148
Desmarestia (Lamour.) Grev.	99
aculeata (L.) Lamour.	99
Desmarestiaceæ Thur.	99
Desmia aculeata Lyngb.	99
Desmotrichum Kütz.	98
undulatum (J. Ag.) Rke.	98
Dichloria Grev.	100
viridis [Müll.] Grev.	100
Dichothrix Zanard.	163
gypsophila [Kütz.] Br et Fl.	163
Dictyosiphon (Grev.) Aresch.	108

Dictyosiphon chordaria Ares. 103
  corymbosus Kjellm. . . 108
  foeniculaceus [Huds.] Grev. 105
    f. flaccida Aresch. . . 105
    var. *subarticulatus* Ar. 101
  foeniculaceus a Aresch. 105
  foeniculaceus b. Aresch. 101
  fragilis Harv. 104
  hippuroides [Lyngb.] Kütz. 105
    f. *fragilis* Kjellm. . . 104
  hispidus Kjellm. . . . 106
  tortilis Gobi 101
Dictyosiphoneæ Thur. . . . 101
Diploderma Kjellm. 56
  amplissimum Kjellm. . 56
    f. planiuscula Fosl. . 56
    f. tenuissima Strf. (Fosl.) 56
    f. typica 56
  miniatum (Ag.) Kjellm. . 57
  tenuissimum Strömf. . . 56
Diplonema Kjellm. 126
  confervoideum [Lgb.] Rke 126
Dumontia [Lam.] J. G. Ag. 37
  filiformis [Fl. Dan.] Grev 37
    f. crispata Grev. . . 37
    f. typica 37
  ramentacea Aresch. . . 35
Dumontiaceæ J. G. Ag. . . 34
Ectocarpaceæ [Ag.] Thur. . 108
Ectocarpus [Lyngb.] Kjellm. 109
  confervoides [Roth.] Le Jol. 109
    f. arcta [Kütz.] Kjellm. 109
    f. penicillata Ag. . . 110
    f. siliculosa [Dillw.] Kjll. 109
    f. typica Kjellm. . . 109
  fasciculatus Harv. . , . 110
  firmus Aresch. . . . 112
  litoralis auct. 112
  repens Rke. 111
  reptans Kjellm. . . . 111

Ectocarpus silienlosus auct. . 109
  sphærophorus auct. . . 103
  terminalis Kütz. 111
Elachista Duby 93
  fucicola [Vell.] Aresch. . 93
  lubrica Rupr. 93
Elachistaceæ Rke. 92
Endoderma Lagerh. 147
  Wittrockii [Wille] Lagerh. 147
Enteromorpha [Link] Harv. 119
  clathrata [Roth] Grev. 120
  clathrata Aresch. . . 120
  complanata Kütz. . . . 123
    f. subsimplex [Aresch.]
      Ahln. 123
  compressa [L.] Ahln. . . 122
    f. racemosa Ahln. . . 123
    f. typica 122
  crinita (Roth) J. G. Ag. 120
  erecta [Lyngb.] J. G. Ag. 120
  intestinalis [L.] Link. . 121
    f. attenuata Ahln. . . 121
    β *clavata* J. G. Ag. . 121
    f. cornucopiæ Lyngb. 121
    α cylindracea J. G. Ag. 121
    f. genuina Ahln . . . 121
    f. *longissima* Aresch. 121
    var. *pumila* Aresch. . 122
  micrococca Kütz. . . . 124
    f. obconica J. G. Ag. . 124
    f. tortuosa J. G. Ag. 124
  microphylla Fosl. . . . 124
  percursa auct. 126
  plumosa Ahln. 123
  prolifera [Müll.] J. Ag 125
  radiata J. G. Ag. . . 120
  tubulosa Kütz. 125
  tubulosa b. *pilifera* Ahln. 125
  usneoides [Bonn.] J. Ag. 123
Entocladia Wittrockii Wille 147

Entophysalis Kütz.	170	Fucus filiformis	
granulosa Kütz.	170	f. Gmelini J. G. Ag.	68
Erythroconis litoralis Oerst.	172	f. Pylaisæi J. G. Ag.	68
Eshara papyracea Ström.	33	*filum* Gunn.	86
Eudesme J. G. Ag.	90	*foliaceus* Ström.	29
virescens |Carm.| J. G. Ag.	90	*fungularis* Fl. Dan.	89
Euthora J. G. Ag.	26	*furcellatus* Gunn.	38
cristata |L.| J. G. Ag.	26	*gigartinus* Gunn.	26
f. angustata Lyngb.	26	*hyperboreus* Gunn.	80
f. typica	26	inflatus L; Vahl	67
Florideæ |Lamour.| Thur.	5	f. latifrons Fosl.	67
Fucaceæ |Ag.| J. G. Ag.	63	f. typica	67
Fucodium canaliculatum J. Ag.	70	*laciniatus* Gunn	25
nodosum J. G. Ag.	64	linearis Fl. Dan.	68
Fucoideæ |Ag.| J. G. Ag.	63	*lumbricalis* β Wg.	38
Fucus |Tourn| Desne et Thur.	64	*lycopodioides* auct.	14
alatus auct.	21	*mamillosus* auct.	32
albus Gunn.	32	miclonensis De la Pyl.	68
Areschougii Kjellm.	66	*muscoides* Gunn.	100
barbatus Gunn.	35	*norvegicus* Gunn.	33
bifurcatus Gunn.	82	*orinus* Gunn.	28
bullatus Fl. Dan.	29	*palmatus* Gunn.	28
caprinus Gunn.	21	*pinnatifidus* Gunn.	12
caprinus Fl. Dan.	29	*plicatus* Wg.	32
cartilagineus Gunn.	41	*plumosus* α et β Wg.	41
„ vindicatus Gunn.	41	*plumosus* γ *tenerrimus* Wg.	42
ciliatus Gunn.	25	*ptilotus* Gunn.	41
coccineus pusillus Wg.	26	*pumilus* Fl. Dan.	25
confervoides auct.	30	*roseus* Fl. Dan.	23
cristatus Sommerf.	26	*rubescens* Sommerf.	99
delicatulus Fl. Dan.	29	*sanguineus* auct.	24
dentatus Gunn.	12	serratus L.	64
distichus L.	69	f. angusta Kjellm.	64
var. *miclonensis* Kleen	68	f. grandifrons Kjellm.	64
f. robustior J. G. Ag.	69	f. typica Kjellm.	64
f. tenuior J. G. Ag.	69	*sinuosus* Wg.	23
divaricatus Gunn.	66	*soboliferus* |Fl. Dan.|	28
elongatus Gunn.	30	*spermophorus* Gunn.	32
excisus auct.	70	spiralis L.	66
filiformis Gmel.	68	f. borealis Kjellm.	66

Fucus subfuscus auct.	14	Haplospora Kjellm.	70
vesiculosus L.	65	globosa Kjellm.	70
f. angustifrons Gobi	65	Hildbrandtia Kütz.	54
f. sphærocarpa J. G. Ag.	66	rosea Kütz.	54
f. subfusiformis Kjellm.	66	Hildbrandtiaceæ Hauck	54
f. turgida Kjellm.	66	*Hormiscia flacca* Aresch.	144
f. typica	65	*Hutchinsia fastigiata* Sommerf.	18
f. vadorum Aresch.	65	nigrescens pectinata Ag.	20
virgatus Gunn.	99	roseola Ag.	16
Furcellaria Lamour.	38	urceolata Lyngb.	16
fastigiata (L.) Lamour	38	Hydrolapathum [Stackh.] J. G. Ag.	24
rotunda Sommerf.	21	sanguineum (L.) Stackh.	24
Furcellariaceæ J. G. Ag.	38	Hypheothrix Kütz.	166
Gastridium filiforme Sommerf.	87	litoralis Hansg.	166
Gigartina (Lamour.) J. G. Ag.	32	*Hypnea purpurascens* Harv.	30
lycopodioides Lyngb.	14	*Ilea fascia* auct.	95
mamillosa (G. et W.) J. Ag.	32	Isthmoplea Kjellm.	108
viridis Lyngb.	100	sphærophora Kjellm.	108
Gigartinaceæ (Kütz.) J. G. Ag.	30	Kallymenia J. G. Ag.	31
Gloeocapsa [Kütz.] Näg.	170	reniformis Kleen	31
crepidinum Thur	170	septemtrionalis Kjellm.	31
Gloeocystis Näg.	155	Laminaria (Lamour.) J. G. Ag.	76
scopulorum Hansg.	155	*Agardhii* Kjellm.	77
Gobia Rke.	102	caperata auct.	77
baltica [Gobi] Rke.	102, 173	*Cloustoni* auct.	80
Gymnogongrus plicatus Harv.	32	cucullata Fosl.	85
Hafgygia Cloustoni Aresch.	80	dermatodea De la Pyl.	74
Halicoccus nodosus Aresch.	64	digitata (L.) Edm.	81
Halidrys [Lyngb.] Grev.	63	f. complanata Kjellm.	81
nodosa Lyngb.	64	f. ensifolia Le Jol.	82
siliquosa [L.] Lyngb.	63	f. genuina Le Jol.	81
Halosaccion (Kütz.) Rupr.	34	f. grandifolia Fosl.	81
pubescens Fosl.	36	f. *longifolia* Fosl.	80
ramentaceum [L.] J. G. Ag.	34	f. stenophylla Harv.	82
f. ramosa Kjellm.	34	f. valida Fosl.	81
α major Kjellm.	34	f. *typica* Fosl.	82
β minor Kjellm.	34	digitata Kleen	82
f. densa Kjellm.	35	digitata Kjellm.	82, 85
f. robusta Kjellm.	34	digitata b. *integrifolia* J. Ag.	85
f. subsimplex Rupr.	35	digitata b. Aresch.	85

Laminaria fascia auct. . . 95
  flexicaulis c. cucull. Le Jol. 85
  flexicaulis d. *ensifolia* L. J. 82
  flexicaulis f. *latilaciniata* 85
  flexicaulis f. *valida* Fosl. 81
  Gunneri Fosl. 79
  hyperborea (Gunn.) Fosl. 80
    f. compressa Fosl. . 80
    f. typica Fosl. . . . 80
    intermedia Fosl. . . . 85
    f. cucullata (Le Jol.) Fosl. 85
    f. longipes Fosl. . . 85
  lorea Aresch. 74
  nigripes J. G. Ag. . . 78
  Pylaii De la Pyl. . . 71
  saccharina (L.) Lamour. 76
    f. Agardhii Kjellm. (Fosl.) 77
    f. borealis Fosl. . . 77
    f. *latissima* Kjellm. . 77
    f linearis J. G. Ag. . 76
    f. longissima (Gun.) Fosl. 77
    f. oblonga J. G. Ag. 77
    stenophylla auct. . . . 82
Laminarieæ (Ag.) Thur. . 71
Leathesia (Gray.) J. G. Ag. 91
  difformis (L.) Aresch. . 91
  marina J. G. Ag. . . 91
Leibleinia confervicola Aresch. 161
  zostericola Aresch. . . 161
Leptochæte Borzi. 160
  marina Hansg. 160
Leptochæteæ Born. et Flah. 160
Leptonema Rke. 93
  fasciculatum Rke. . . 93
  f. majus Rke. . . . 93
Leptothrix Kütz. 171
  arctica Fosl. 171
  subtilissima Hansg. . . 171
Lithoderma Aresch. . . . 92
  fatisceus Aresch. . . . 92

Lithodermaceæ Hauck . . . 92
Lithophyllum (Phil.) Rosan. . 9
  læve Strömf. 10
  Lenormandi (Aresch.) Rosan. 9
  zonatum Fosl 10
Lithothamnion Phil. 6
  byssoides Unger . . . 8
  calcareum var. *norvegicum*
    Aresch. 6
  circumscriptum Strömf. . 9
  flavescens Kjellm. . . . 8
  glaciale Kjellm 7
  intermedium Kjellm. . . 7
  norvegicum Aresch. (Kjellm.) 6
  polymorphum (L.) Aresch. 9
  soriferum Kjellm. . . 6
  Ungeri Kjellm. 8
Lyngbya [Ag.] Thur. . . . 165
  inundata (Kütz.) Hansg. 166
  jadertina (Menegh.) Hausg. 165
  luteo-fusca (Ag.) J. G. Ag. 165
  semiplena (Ag.) J. G. Ag. 165
Mastichotricheæ Kütz. . . . 161
Mastigonema velutinum Wolle 162
Melobesia (Lamour.) Rosan. . 11
  Lenormandi auct . . . 9
  macrocarpa Rosan. . . 11
Merismopedia litoralis Warm. 172
Mesogloia virescens auct. . . 90
Micrococcus Cohn 172
  sordidus Schröt. . . . 172
  f. marina Hansg. . . 172
Monostroma [Thur.] Wittr. . 113
  angicava Kjellm. . . . 116
  arcticum Wittr. . . . 118
  Blyttii [Aresch.] Wittr. . 119
  cylindraceum Kjellm. . 116
  fuscum [P. et R.] Wittr. 118
  latissimum [Kütz.] Wittr. 114
  pulchrum Farl. 114

Monostroma saccodeum Kjellm.	116	Phyllaria Le Jol.	74
f. cylindracea Kjll. (Fosl)	116	dermatodea (De la Pyl.) L. J.	74
f. typica	116	f. lanceolata Fosl.	74
undulatum Wittr.	114	f. oblonga Fosl.	75
f. Farlowii Fosl.	114	Phyllitis [Kütz] Le Jol.	95
f. typica Fosl.	114	cæspitosa auct.	95
Myrionema Grev.	91	fascia (Müll.) Kütz.	95
strangulans Grev.	91	Phyllophora (Grev.) J. G. Ag.	31
vulgare auct.	92	Brodiæi (Turn.) J. G. Ag.	31
Myrionemaceæ [Thur.]	91	Physematoplea Kjellm.	97
Nostoc Vauch	164	attenuata Kjellm.	97
maculiforme Born. et Flah.	164	Pilinia Kütz.	146
f. norvegica Hansg.	164	minor Hansg.	146
Nostocaceæ [Kütz.] Thur.	163	Pleurocapsa Thur	168
Nodularia Mert.	164	fuliginosa Hauck	168
spumigena Mer.	164	Pleurococcus [Menegh.] Näg.	158
f. litorea [Kütz.] Born. et Flah.	164	marinus Hansg.	158
		f. major	158
Odonthalia Lyngb.	12	f. typica	158
dentata (L.) Lyngb.	12	Polycystis Kütz.	169
Orgyia pinnata Gobi	72	litoralis Hansg.	169
Oscillaria (Bosc.) Thur.	167	Polyides Ag.	21
conferricola Lyngb.	161	lumbricalis J. G. Ag.	21
neapolitana Kütz.	167	rotundus (Gmel.) Grev.	21
scopulorum Lyngb.	162	Polysiphonia Grev.	15
zostericola Lyngb.	161	arctica J. G. Ag.	19
Oscillariaceæ (Ag.) Wittr.	165	Brodiæi Aresch.	20
Ozothallia Desne. et Thur.	63	fastigiata [Roth] Grev.	18
nodosa (L.) Desne. et Thur.	64	nigrescens (Huds.) Harv.	20
Palmella [Lyngb.] Näg.	157	f. pectinata Ag.	20
mediterranea Kütz.	157	urceolata [Lightf.] Grev.	15
Palmellaceæ [Desne.] Näg.	155	f. comosa Ag [J. G. Ag.]	16
Pelvetia Desne. et Thur.	69	f. formosa Suhr. [J. G. Ag.]	16
canaliculata [L.] Des. et Th.	70	f. patens (Dillw.) J. G. Ag.	15
Petrocelis J. G. Ag.	55	α distans Fosl.	16
Middendorffi [Rupr.] Kjellm.	55	β fasciculata Fosl.	16
Phloeospora Aresch.	101	f. roseola Ag. (J. G. Ag.)	16
subarticulata Aresch.	101	f. typica	15
tortilis (Rupr.) Aresch.	101	Porphyra Ag.	58
Phycochromophyceæ Rabenh.	160	abyssicola Kjellm.	60

Porphyra coccinea Kleen	56	*Pylaiella litoralis* [L.] Kjellm	112
laciniata [Lightf.] Ag.	58	macrocarpa Fosl.	112
f. *linearis* Kleen	56	varia Kjellm.	113
f. typica	59	*Ralfsia* Berk.	89
f. umbilicalis L. (Kleen)	59	densta [Ag.] J. G. Ag.	89
f. *vulgaris* Kleen	56	Ralfsiaceæ Farl.	89
miniata Aresch.	56	*Rhizoclonium* Kütz.	138
miniata Collins	56	rigidum Gobi	140
vulgaris Aresch.	59	riparium [Roth] Harv.	138
Porphyraceæ [Kütz.] Thur.	56	f. pannosa [Aresch.] Fosl.	139
Prasiola [Ag.] Jess.	127	f. typica Wittr	138
furfuracea [Mert.] Menegh.	127	f. valida Fosl.	138
Lenormandiana Suhr.	127	*Rhodochorton* Näg.	48
leprosa auct.	127	mesocarpum [Carm.] Kjellm.	50
stipitata Suhr.	128	f. penicilliformis Kjellm.	50
Protococcaceæ [Menegh.]	159	Rothii Turt.[Näg.	48
Protococcus [Ag] Rabenh.	159	f globosa Kjellm.	48
marinus Kütz.	159	f. typica	48
f. Foslieana Hansg.	159	sparsum [Carm.] Kjellm.	49
ovalis Hansg.	159	*Rhodomela* [Ag.] J. G. Ag.	13
Ptilota [Ag.] J. G. Ag.	40	*gracilis* Kleen	20
elegans Bonnem.	40	lycopodioides [L] Ag.	13
pectinata (Gunn.) Kjellm.	42	f. cladostephus J. G. Ag.	
f Kjellmani Fosl.	42	[Kjellm.]	13
f. *litoralis* Kjellm.	42	α densa Kjellm.	13
f. typica	42	f. flagellaris Kjellm.	14
α distans Fosl.	42	f typica	13
β densa Fosl.	42	α compacta Kjellm.	13
plumosa [L.] Ag.	41	β laxa Kjellm.	13
plumosa asplenoides Lgb.	42	γ tenera Kjellm.	13
sericea Harv.	40	Rhodomelaceæ J. G. Ag.	12
serrata auct.	42	*Rhodophyllis* Kütz.	25
Punctaria Grev.	98	dichotoma [Lepech.] Gobi	25
plantaginea [Roth] Grev.	98	*reprecula* auct.	25
f. linearis Fosl.	99	*Rhodymenia* [Grev.] J. G Ag.	27
f typica	98	cristata auct.	26
undulata J. G. Ag.	98	mamillosa Aresch.	33
Punctariaceæ	98	palmata [L.] Grev.	27
Pylaiella Bory	111	f. angustifolia Kjellm.	28
curta Fosl.	111	f. prolifera Kütz.	28

Rhodymenia palmata
  f. sarniensis [Mert., Grev.   28
  α latiuscula Kjel'm.   28
  β tenuissima Tourn.   28
  f. sobolifera [Fl. Dan.] Harv. 28
  f. typica   27
  α nuda Kjellm   27
  β marginifera [Turn.] Hrv. 28
Rhodymeniaceæ [Harv.] J. Ag.   24
Rivulariaceæ [Harv.] Born. et Flah. 160
Saccorhiza dermatodea auct.   74
Sarcina Goods.   172
  litoralis [Oerst.] Pouls   172
  f. norvegica Hansg.   172
Schizogonium Kütz.   128
  radicans [Kütz.] Gay.   128
Schizomycetes Cohn   171
Schizophyceæ Cohn   160
Scytosiphon [Ag.] Thur   96
  attenuatus Kjellm.   97
  compressus γ confervoides Lyngb.   126
  erectus Lyngb.   120
  foeniculaceus Lyngb.   105
  hippuroides Lyngb.   105
  intestinalis γ cornucopiæ Lyngb.   121
  lomentarius [Lyngb.] J. Ag.   96
  f. fistulosa [Ag.]   96
  f. typica   96
  ramentaceus Lyngb.   35
Scytosiphoneæ Thur.   95
Sphacelaria [Lyngb.] J. G. Ag. 107
  arctica auct.   107
  olivacea [Dillw.] Ag.   108
  plumosa auct.   106
  racemosa Grev.   107
  f. arctica [Harv.] Rke.   107
Sphacelariaceæ J. G. Ag.   106

Sphærococcus cristatus β angustatus Lyngb.   26
  mamillosus Sommerf.   33
  sarniensis Kütz.   28
Spirulina Turp.   167
  tenuissima Kütz.   167
Spongomorpha Kütz.   129
  arcta [Dillw.] Kütz.   130
  f hystrix Strömf. [Fosl.] 131
  f. penicilliformis Fosl.   131
  f. pulvinata Fosl.   130
  f. Sonderi Kütz. [Fosl.] 131
  f. typica Fosl.   130
  hystrix Strömf.   131
  intermedia Fosl.   133
  lanosa [Roth] Kütz.   133
  f. typica   133
  f. uncialis [F. Dan.] Thur. 134
  minima Fosl.   134
  spinescens Kütz.   130
  villosa auct.   134
Spongiocarpeæ Grev.   20
Squamariaceæ (Zanard.) Hauck 55
Thamnidium mesocarpum f. penicilliformis Kjellm.   50
  Rothii auct.   48
  sparsum Kleen   49
Tetranema percursum Aresch. 126
Tilopterideæ Thur.   70
Trentepohlia virgatula Farl.   51
  secundata Aresch.   53
Ulothrichaceæ [Rabenh.]   143
Ulothrix Kütz.   143
  discifera Kjellm.   129
  flacca [Dillw.] Thür.   144
  implexa Kütz.   143
  radicans Kütz.   129
Ulva [L.] Wittr.   119
  Blyttii Aresch.   119
  caprina Gunn.   29

Ulva compressa Wg.	122	*Ulva sobolifera* auct.	29
var. *subsimplex* Aresch.	123	*sobolifera* Gunn.	35
delicatula Gunn.	29	*sordida* Aresch.	118
fascia Lyngb.	95	*umbilicalis* auct.	59
filiformis auct.	37	β *purpurea* Wg.	56
intestinalis Gunn.	122	Ulvaceæ [Ag.] Rke.	113
intestinalis var. *nana* Smft.	124	Urococcus Hass.	156
lactuca L.	119	Foslicanus Hausg.	156
lactuca Wg.	114	Urospora Aresch.	145
latissima Gunn.	77	penicilliformis [Roth]	
latissima Kleen.	119	Aresch.	144, 145
longissima Gunn.	77	Vaucheria D. C.	148
maxima Gunn.	77	coronata Nordst.	148
palmata Lyngb.	29	*marina* Lyngb.	149
percursa Sommerf.	126	*pusilla* Lyngb.	151
plantaginifolia Lyngb.	98	Vaucheriaceæ [Gray] Dum.	148
rigida Sommerf.	119	*Wormskioldia sanguinea* Kleen.	24
rubescens auct.	99	Wrangeliaceæ [J. G. Ag.] Hauck.	50

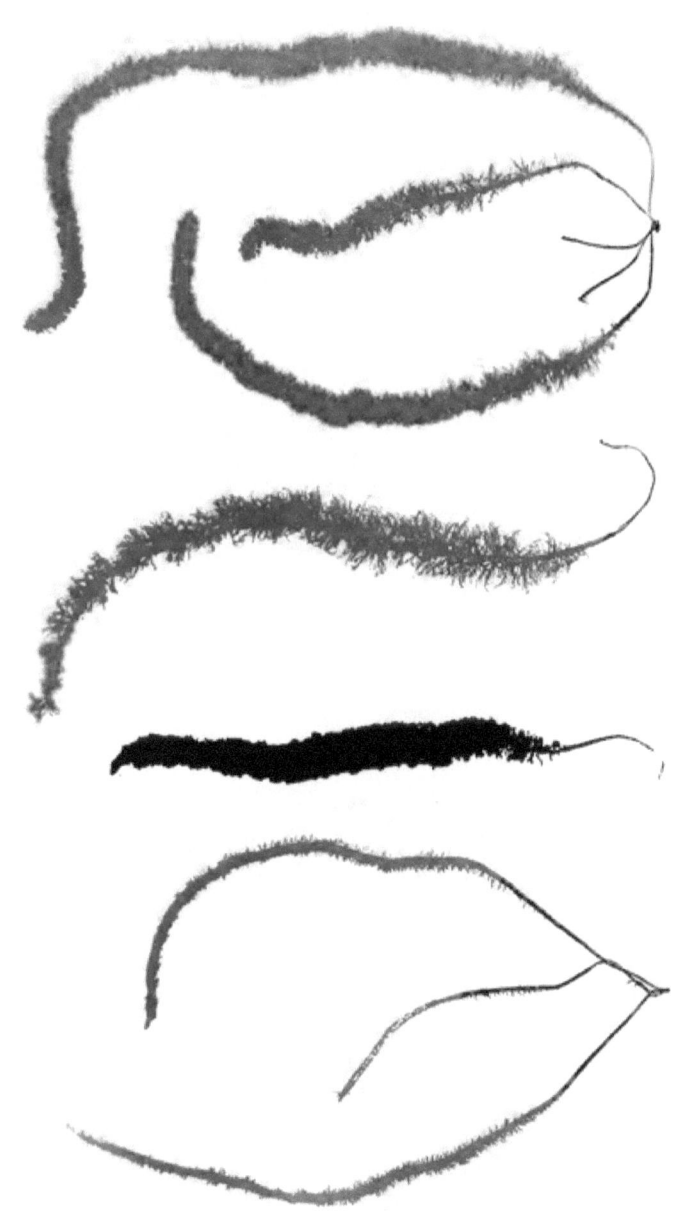

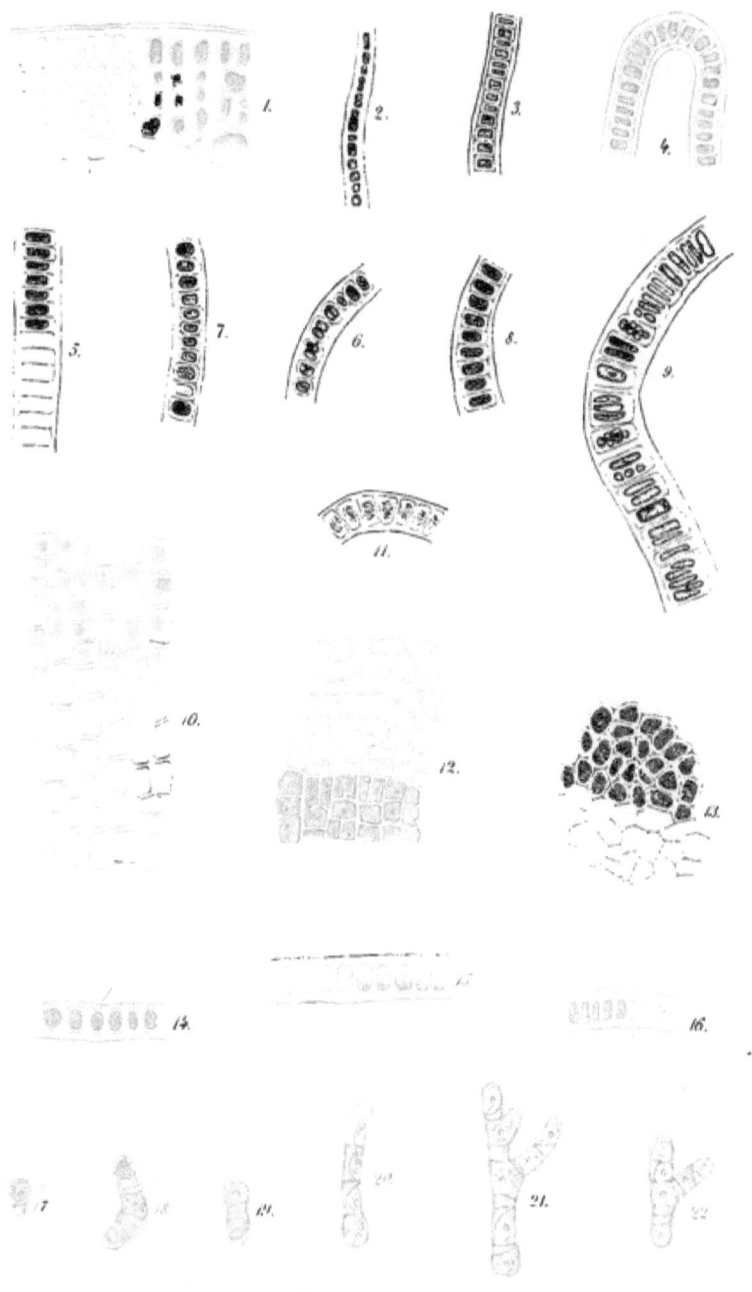

Foslie. Contribution I. Pl. 2.

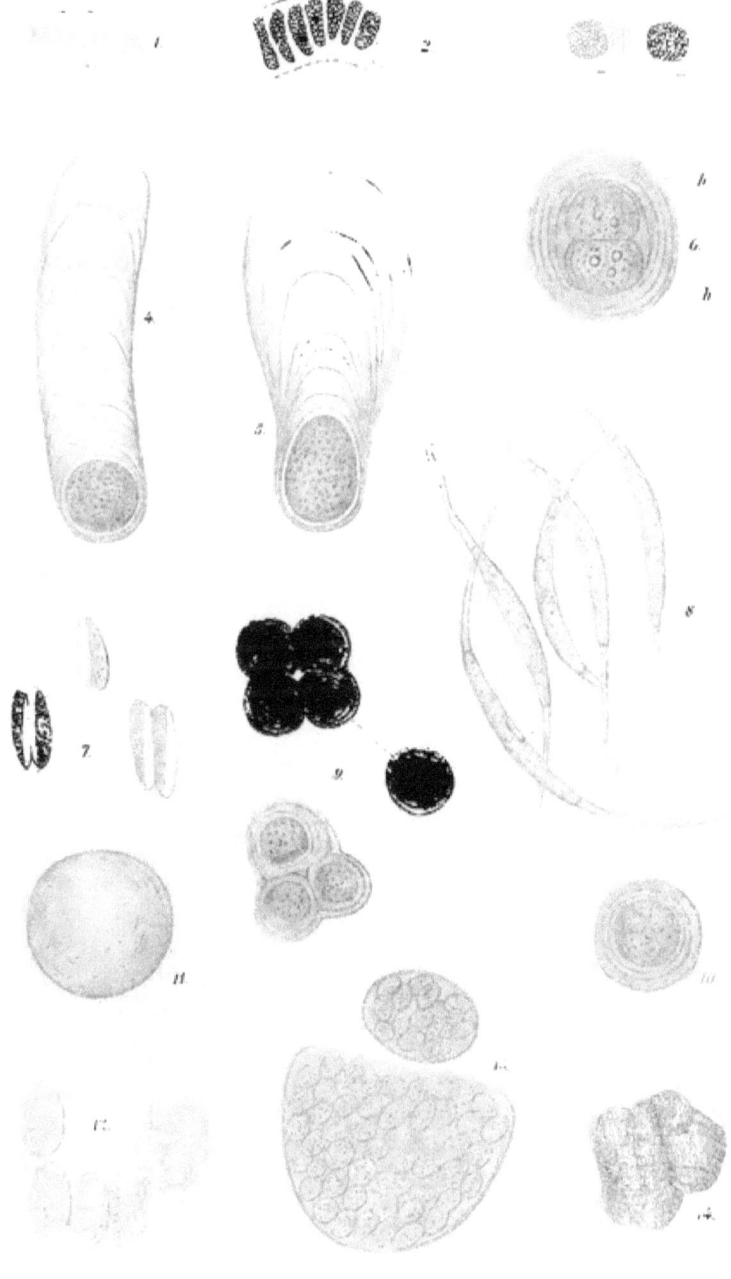

www.ingramcontent.com/pod-product-compliance
Lightning Source LLC
Chambersburg PA
CBHW030818190426
43197CB00036B/597